FLAMENCO
...All You Wanted to Know
by Emma Martínez

Cover photo of Paco de Lucía courtesy of Amelia Martínez. Used by permission De Lucía Gestion S.L.

1 2 3 4 5 6 7 8 9 0

Visit us on the Web at www.melbay.com — E-mail us at email@melbay.com

FLAMENCO
...All You Wanted to Know

INTRODUCTION

Si hay un arte que sabe que vivimos solo una vez y que la vida es cruel, es el flamenco.- Felix Grande

"If there is an art form which knows that we only live once and that life is cruel, that art is flamenco."

- Felix Grande.

Flamenco is the supreme art of the individual; each interpreter's personality, character and life experience come out in their song, their dance, their playing. Flamenco music is not just music, the singing is not just a song, the dance is not just a dance. In performance, flamenco is like a miniature opera, except that the libretto has been written by history, and each performer interprets it from their own perspective of it. Flamenco touches on the philosophical questions of life, all of the 'human condition' is there; solitude, suffering, love, joy, passion and death. The miracle is how it expresses all of this. A dancer's small gesture can speak volumes; how she reaches her arm to pluck the invisible orange blossom and draw it into the perfumed fold of her arms and breast. A *cantaor*,[1] in a single stifled cry can communicate a lifetime of longing; squeezing his arms to his sides as though holding in the uncontainable, stretching out his open hands in supplication. It's an art filled with gestures whose meanings are enigmatic and open to interpretation. It's a living art with its own dialect, traditions and rules dating back to the 1700s. It's a way of life, a way of perceiving and interpreting daily existence and because of this it's in a permanent state of evolution.

Ottmar Liebert's 1990 CD *Nouveau Flamenco* is sold with a sticker declaring it to be: "The classic album that defined a new category of music." *Nouveau* is French for 'new' and Flamenco is the Spanish term for a style of music which has no French connections nor heritage. The most recent developments in flamenco, overwhelmingly influenced by Paco de Lucía have been dubbed *Nuevo Flamenco*. Perhaps *Nouveau Flamenco* is not the same as *Nuevo Flamenco*, indeed what Ottmar Liebert plays is not flamenco, but how can you tell since you've been told it *is* flamenco by both the record company and the store where you bought it? The Californian duo of Willi and Lobo's CD (Narada 2000) is sold with a label that declares it to be a: "World Music carnival of exotic Gypsy Flamenco sounds from Cuba, the Caribbean and the Western shores of Mexico." What is a World Music Carnival? Does it have anything to do with flamenco? Are there Flamenco Gypsies from Cuba, the Caribbean and Western Mexico? Do Spanish aficionados listen to these musicians, and if not, why not?

Flamenco music encompasses such a broad spectrum of sounds and influences today, that it's difficult for anyone coming to it for the first time to tell what is old or new or simply, what *is* flamenco? Musicians from other disciplines, like easy listening or middle-of-the-road jazz and pop, classical and even heavy rock artists are choosing a little element of the style and adding it to their repertoire: often a characteristic rhythm, or a few exotic sounding guitar chords is enough to classify their 'new' music as flamenco. How can the uninitiated be sure they're getting the real thing? How do you recognise flamenco and get to the essence? Is it Ottmar Leibert, The Gypsy Kings, Manitas de Plata, Joaquin Cortés, Los Chichos, Los Nuevos Flamencos ....?

---

[1]Exclusive term for a flamenco singer

CHAPTER 1: WHAT IS FLAMENCO?

When you go to see a flamenco production, everything you're witnessing, the singer, the dancer, the guitar solos, all stem from one source: flamenco song- *El Cante*. Recent investigators have begun uncovering the evolution of these song and dance forms-practically each song has a corresponding dance- and most now assume that before the different song styles were defined, flamenco originated in the dances, which were always accompanied by song. But as everything we know as flamenco today has evolved gradually over time, we can't pinpoint one particular style of dance or song as being the first. What we can be sure of though, is that everything in flamenco is related, like an extended family, and that there are no hard and fast rules. With every aspect of flamenco three magic words should always be attached to any categorical statement: *but not always.*

THE FLAMENCO TRIUMVIRATE

The roots of flamenco are in the songs- *cantes*- with names like *soleares, tarantos, seguirilla, tientos,* and many more. These names refer to a musical *pattern*: flamenco is basically a set of songs and corresponding dances which are identified by their patterns: patterns of rhythm, of harmony and you could even say also emotional patterns. Every flamenco song has a traditional emotional theme[2] and each song type belongs to a 'family' pattern. The *soleares* family, for example, which all share the same rhythm and emotional themes, or the *fandangos* family, which share the same harmonic progressions; there's a family of *tangos* and *cantiñas* or the *malagueñas* family, and the small family of cantes which have no musical accompaniment, called *cantes a palo seco*- "dry song styles." The song patterns, along with *El Baile* - flamenco dance- and *La Guitarra*, form the foundation pillars of the art of flamenco, a kind of triumvirate which has evolved to produce the solo concert flamenco guitar, and more recently flamenco-style percussion.

The rhythmic pattern of a given flamenco song is called the *compás*- which is like the skeleton on which it's built. Most cantes also have a particular musical key with a specific harmonic structure. Most of these characteristics are disguised by the spontaneous and highly individualistic delivery of each performer, which makes flamenco look improvised.[3] Anybody playing flamenco is playing one of these specific patterns known as *palos* or *formas* and each performance of flamenco is a recreation of a traditional flamenco pattern or style, just as classical music is a performer's interpretation of a composer's piece.

There are three fundamental elements which can help define whether or not something really is flamenco: A flamenco mode -or musical tonality-; the *compás* -rhythm- and the performer himself who should be a Flamenco! All three of these elements: tonality, *compás*, a flamenco performer and then something less easily identifiable- *Flamencura*- must be present together if we are to end up with a piece of music which can be labelled 'flamenco'. By themselves, these elements won't turn a piece of music into flamenco. For example, if a composer writes a song using a flamenco key- usually called a mode- he won't be writing a flamenco piece. If he writes another piece using an identifiable rhythmic cycle -*compás*- that won't make it flamenco either. And if a flamenco singer from a traditionally flamenco family sings a song by Frank Sinatra, that won't make it flamenco!

---

[2]See Chapter 6, "What Are They Singing About?"
[3]See Chapter 8, "Are They Improvising?"

FLAMENCO FORMS: The Palos

The names for the song patterns are unique to flamenco. Sometimes they're simply an Andalucian pronunciation of a Spanish word which describes the mood conveyed by the song. For example the *soleá* (also in the plural *soleares*), is thought to come from the Andalucian pronunciation of the word *soledad*, solitude. It's the name for a song form often used by guitarists to teach beginners, because its rhythmic pattern, a cycle of 12 beats with accents on the third, 6th, 8th, 10th and 12th beats, is also the same rhythmic basis for other flamenco forms, like the *bulerías* and *alegrías*. Once you've got the hang of the soleares form, you can move onto the *alegrías* and *bulerías*.

In recital, a singer will often announce what style he's going to sing by saying: "Now I'm going to sing a little *por alegrías*." which means he will be singing in the *compás* and harmony, as well as the emotional context of an *alegrías*. When you refer to a performance of a flamenco style, you say someone played *por tangos*, or *por bulerías; in the style of* a *tangos*, or *bulerías*. Just as you might say a band played a waltz, tango or a milonga, without specifying who wrote it, or whose version it was.

There are several different versions of each style. Sometimes they're named after the village or town where they developed, such as the Soleá de Alcalá which is named after the town outside the city of Seville, Alcalá de Guadaira. Others are named after the singer who made them famous or developed them, like the *Malagueñas del Mellizo*, - a *malagueñas* song the cantaor from Cádiz, Enrique El Mellizo invented (Enrique The Twin, 1848-1906). Or the *Tangos del Titi* which are named after El Titi de Triana- a singer from Seville who was well known for his interpretation of the *tangos* style. So the singer is saying he's going to be singing *in the style of* the particular form, but he doesn't always say exactly which version he'll do. And even within this variety there are stylistic differences which make for an infinite variety of interpretations. Each singer brings his or her own personality and inventiveness to their song, within the outlines of the style. They improvise small differences which make every performance unique and unrepeatable.

THE PERFORMER: *Flamencura*

Anyone who spends time with a group of Flamencos, professionals or amateurs, will experience their *forma de ser*, their way of being. In this way flamenco is comparable to the blues and jazz, which have a similar history and evolution, and whose fans have a similar outlook. When a Flamenco is described as being *flamenco hasta el andar* (flamenco even in the way he walks), it sums this up. *Aficionados*[4] will talk about a particular *cantaor's* style and emotional involvement as *su cante*- his song, and distinguish each interpretation of a *seguiriya* or a *solea* as: *su cante por seguiriya* or *su cante por solea*. A singer is judged on his emotional sincerity, how well he or she knows the intricacies of the style they're performing and their feeling for the *compás*. In a word, their *flamencura*. When performed by gifted *cantaors*, professional or otherwise, flamenco produces some of the most profound and emotionally charged moments you'll find in any music. A good singer will literally bare his soul, the finesse, tonal accuracy and degree of vocal technique are not as important as their *flamencura*. Whether they make the hair stand up on the back of your neck is basically all that counts.

THE COMPÁS

The *compás* is a rhythmic cycle, a recurring pattern, with accents in certain places. A common cycle in several different palos is one of 12 beats. The same term- compás- is used in classical music, (and jazz) but not with the same meaning: *compás* means a bar, (a measure) of written music. In English you say a measure in

---

[4]Enthusiasts

4/4 or a measure in 6/8, in Spanish you say a *compás* in 4/4 etc. In flamenco to be in *compás*, doesn't just mean you are playing to a particular count, it means you accent the beat within the cycle in the right place, and feel the rhythm so well, that you are able to stretch it and bend it and yet never stray out of it. Each song has a specific emotional content or theme, the words define the feelings in each *palo*, and the *compás* is intimately tied up with this. So when Flamencos talk about being *in compás*, it's more than just playing in time, it's about being in the right emotional 'place' as well.

The *compás* is cyclical, but how fast or slow and what emphasis each interpreter gives makes for an infinite variety of 'versions' of each *palo*. The sense of *compás* in Jerez is different than the sense of *compás* in Lebrija or Morón, Seville or Cádiz, all rich traditional flamenco areas. As you listen to singers and guitarists from these places, so you'll begin to distinguish the slower pace of Lebrija, the driving force of Jerez, the infectious catchiness of Cádiz, and the lightness of Seville.

It's a sin to be found 'out of *compás*'. For people coming to flamenco for the first time, the cycles sound easy to follow and clap along to, but the clapping- *palmas*- follows it's own cycles inside the rhythm, and can be incredibly complex. Each *compás* is really an amalgam of rhythms, like a cake cut up into pieces, but still forming a whole. Flamencos who have spent their lives playing to these rhythms find it second nature; it's almost impossible for them to stray out of *compás*. For Spanish Flamencos, being in *compás* or not, or even asking "what *compás* is it in?" simply doesn't occur to them, it comes as naturally as walking.

There is nothing worse than watching someone play flamenco while they're actually counting the *compás*. It ruins the possibility of building atmosphere or tension, because everybody ends up counting, instead of feeling the swing. The Gypsy flamenco guitarist Raimundo Amador,[5] (who has performed with B.B. King and the Icelandic pop singer Björk,) can't help grinding his teeth when he's playing; it seems to be a family trait, since his father does the same thing[6]. He looks like he's got a fixed grin on his face as he chomps along, and people sometimes say he looks like he's laughing while he's playing. Raimundo said: *"It's not that I'm laughing all the time. It's just that I'm keeping compás with my teeth, you know? But I do have a laugh too."*[7]

THE MUSICAL NITTY GRITTY- FLAMENCO MODES- THE KEY

Flamenco music is played in a mixture of keys, both 'standard' which is based on major and minor scales just like most classical and pop music uses- and modal which in Spain can be traced back to the Roman liturgical music of the 11th-13th Centuries. Modes were invented by the Greeks even before this time; they're types of musical scales with names like Dorian, Phrygian or Lydian. A great deal of flamenco music is in the Phrygian mode which in Spain, confusingly, is sometimes called Doric. The Phrygian mode is typical of Greek folk music, it is also common in the folk music of Israel, Arab-influenced Yugoslavia, Bulgaria, Macedonia and eastern Europe. Its use in Spain is unique in Western European folk or popular music. The Flamenco Phrygian mode is not strictly the Greek Phrygian mode because it alters one of its steps, or intervals. Even in this fundamental element flamenco is unique! Modes differ from major and minor scales in the size of their intervals, the spaces between each note. This is easy to visualise on a piano keyboard: it's the distance between two adjacent keys. If there's a black key between two white ones, the interval between the two white keys is major; if no key separates the two the interval is minor. The greater the distance between steps, the greater the musical interval, and the location of these jumps in the order of notes determines whether the whole scale is major or minor. Which mode you choose for a composition governs how the rest of the melody behaves, it

[5]See Chapter 13, "What Is Flamenco Fusion?"
[6]In Carlos Saura's movie 'Flamenco' you can see Raimundo Amador's father accompanying El Chocolate and El Farruco
[7]Raimundo Amador, from Historia Guia del Nuevo Flamenco, Pedro Calvo and J.M Gamboa. Ediciones Guia de Musica 1994

will influence the mood of the piece. A major key invariably sounds jolly, a minor key is more introverted and serious, and the Flamenco Phrygian mode seems to wander about unpredictably between one mood and another. These elements, combined with the compás and the cultural ingredients, give flamenco singing its unique characteristics.

TAKE THE CHORD BY THE HORNS....

One of the outstanding coincidences in the development of flamenco, is that its history coincides exactly with the development of the modern Spanish guitar.[8] Paco de Lucía has called the sequence of guitar chords typical of the majority of flamenco forms the 'Andalucian cadence'. The keys or modes in which flamenco music is played and sung have consistently defied common musical notation or categorisation. These peculiarities are directly related to the peculiar tuning of the guitar, and how the guitarist's fingers fall naturally on the fingerboard to produce the notes in any given chord. This physical peculiarity allows odd notes to creep in where they're not supposed to be, according to the conventional science of harmony. To play chords on the guitar is quite a tricky thing, sometimes a string has to be avoided otherwise it would add a note that doesn't belong to that particular chord, at least, according to the classical theory of harmony. Writing down these flamenco chords in the same way as their strictly classical counterparts, a normal F♯ chord for example, misses the detail which makes it sound flamenco. A flamenco F♯ chord has an extra note which doesn't really belong there, it's this extraneous note that makes it sound flamenco. In strict scientific terms, the Flamenco Phrygian F♯ chord is actually F♯7B911. Somehow it's hard to imagine one flamenco guitarist saying to another: "Hey, it's in F♯7B911!" Much easier to say "Por medio," which indicates the position of the left hand. Like jazz, flamenco is not governed by theory, but by the mood of the moment. This is one reason why writing flamenco music down has always been problematic; because it doesn't fit neatly within the rules laid down by music theory. The flamenco and jazz flute player Jorge Pardo from Paco de Lucía's septet likes to call these flamenco chords 'horned chords',- *con cuernos*- writing them in inverted commas, which look like miniature bull's horns, to indicate they are not strictly what they say they are.

EL CANTE

All flamenco, the singing, dancing and guitar playing, is believed to have evolved from the songs- *El Cante*. There have been very few innovations in the style of singing over the past century or so, the technique and patterns remain the same as they were essentially a hundred years ago. The name for flamenco singing- *el cante*- sometimes called *Cante Jondo*,[9] is a strictly flamenco term. Flamenco has it's own dialect, a jargon which distinguishes it from other musical styles. It is sung by a *cantaor* or *cantaora* a male or female flamenco singer who is usually accompanied by a *tocaor,* a flamenco guitarist. In Spanish, any other style of singer is called a *cantante,* and any other style of song is called *un canto.* So you'll find a description of a flamenco recital giving the names of the performers as so-and-so *'al cante'* (singing), and so-and-so *'al toque'* (on the guitar.) Compared to the other two pillars of the flamenco triumvirate, el cante has remained the most traditional. Lyrics dating from the 1800s are still commonly sung in recitals and recorded on disc, and although verses from more recent poets such as García Lorca have been incorporated, a cantaor is still judged on his knowledge of the traditional lyrics to the cantes.

---

[8] See Chapter 10, "Flamenco Guitar or Spanish Guitar?"
[9] See Chapter 3, "What is Cante Jondo?"

EL BAILE

Which came first, el cante or el baile? is one of those questions in flamenco which rouses hot debate among specialists in Spain. Before the cantes were defined and given set shapes which are always followed in performance, came el baile. Another intriguing question might be; which came first, the verse or the song? Most of the developments in flamenco can be traced back to the mid 1800s, written accounts and anecdotes provide the evidence which suggests that the songs and dances in flamenco as we know it today, evolved together, with some aspects of the art developing and being more popular at times than others. So the early history of flamenco has more famous dancers than famous singers, and today there are arguably more famous guitarists than famous singers. Aficionados of el baile are more likely to claim their speciality as the source of all else, likewise cantaores have a tradition of behaving like the guardians of the Truth in flamenco, declaring that the roots of everything lie in their speciality.

A male flamenco dancer is called a *bailaor*, the female, a *bailaora*. A ballet dancer, or any other style of dancer is referred to as a *bailarín/a*. Within flamenco dance there are patterns of movements which all have their own names: the *escobilla*, *desplante* and *llamada* for example, which are echoed in the flamenco guitar technique where the same terminology is used for certain musical patterns within the form. The differences between the techniques used by male and female dancers have been breaking down more and more over the years, so that there are now male dancers who use their arms as gracefully and expressively as women dancers, and women who can tap their feet in the characteristic zapateado with as much force and speed as the men. Needless to say, this unisex kind of style is constantly argued about in the pages of flamenco journals and reviews. Traditionally the *bailaora* emphasises her upper body with graceful arm movements and gestures, while the man more often displays fierce footwork, and traditionally masculine postures. The dancer Vicente Escudero (1885-1980) drew up his own list of rules for the male flamenco dancer which he called a 'Decálogo', almost like ten commandments mostly relating to posture and gesture which he deemed should always be strictly within a masculine aesthetic. These days there seem to be very few male dancers who understand the difference between masculine and feminine, resulting in all sorts of balletic moves. Many of the successful stars of today's flamenco dance were schooled in ballet technique as well as flamenco which has undoubtedly enriched the art, just as some knowledge of classical techniques enriched the flamenco guitar.[10]

LA GUITARRA

Most non-Spaniards come to flamenco via the guitar or el baile. Today the flamenco guitar has practically overtaken the classical guitar in terms of popularity and even musical inventiveness. Many contemporary flamenco guitarists, firstly Paco de Lucía and the following generation such as Juan Manuel Cañizares, Vicente Amigo, or Rafael Riqueni have produced flamenco 'compositions' which rival those of classical guitarist/composers. The flamenco guitar has been responsible for most of the developments in flamenco generally over the past 50 years or so, as players have started to experiment with influences from outside the strictly flamenco environment, such as Brazilian and jazz harmonies and progressions, and Latin American-tinged rhythms.

As with every other aspect of flamenco, there are specific terms for a guitarist who's called a *guitarrista* or more often a *tocaor*, from the verb *tocar* 'to play'. *Tocar* is used specifically to say 'playing an instrument', the Spanish for play as in 'child's play' is *jugar*. A classical guitarist (also jazz or any other style,) is called a *guitarrista* whether they're male or female.

---

[10]See Chapter 11, "Who Were the Famous Flamenco Guitarists?"

FOREIGN FLAMENCOS

A flamenco performer can come from just about anywhere. The abundance of very good non-Andalucian performers, particularly dancers and guitarists, proves that flamenco can be learned. It's the depth of feeling conveyed, the conviction in the performance- the *flamencura*- which aficionados judge, and these things have to be intuited. Intuition is mostly based on knowledge, whether conscious or subconscious, so growing up in a flamenco environment where a sense of *flamencura* is palpable makes for a greater flamenco intuition. This is more likely to be found in Andalucia than anywhere else in the world. Even though many of today's popular and successful Flamenco's were born and bred in Madrid[11], most of them were raised within a Flamenco ambience, or they sought it themselves in order to develop their talent. Many respectable non-Spanish flamenco performers in both *el baile* and *la guitarra* exist outside Spain, but it's still largely true that in order to sing flamenco one has to be born into it. And to play flamenco convincingly, you have to live and breath it. Although it's possible to learn to play specific techniques and styles, a 'flamenco instinct' is often all we have to distinguish what is flamenco and what is not. And that instinct -*flamencura*- doesn't come shrink wrapped as part of lesson one.

Anybody playing, singing or dancing flamenco is sticking to the *compás*, harmony and mood of the specific styles. So, if a flute player and a violinist get together and play one of these rhythmic forms, is it flamenco? If a singer gets together with a jazz pianist and performs one of them, is it flamenco? Strictly speaking- yes. Just like the 'classical' styles of fugue, passacaglia, waltz or jig, it doesn't matter who plays what instrument, if it follows the basic structure of these styles, that's what it is. But if these performers lack the experience of flamenco as a culture, what they play won't sound convincing. Just as when a classical pianist decides to play jazz, if he ain't got that swing, well ... he just ain't got it. A classical guitarist may interpret a piece by Paco de Lucía, so may a jazz pianist, this essentially means they're playing a flamenco form or composition, it doesn't make them *flamencos*. Yet, any Flamenco performing a style not strictly adhering to the fundamental elements of flamenco may also be deemed to be performing with 'a flamenco air'. A flamenco identity is intricately tied up with Andalucian Gypsy culture and Andalucian society.[12] To be a Flamenco means you have a certain style, an outlook and view of life which affects everything you do–Flamenco even in the way you walk.

WHERE DOES IT COME FROM?

Flamenco comes from Andalucia which is the largest region of Spain, and historically the poorest. Andalucia is made up of eight provinces; Huelva, Sevilla, Cádiz, Jaén, Málaga, Almería, Granada and Córdoba. Although flamenco is played in many parts of the region, the cities of Cádiz, Sevilla, Jerez and Huelva all claim to be the birthplace of flamenco. The area these cities/provinces form (each is the capital of its province) around the basin of the Guadalquivir River, is sometimes called Lower Andalucia–*Bajo Andalucia*. Just as the French tradition for wine making has produced some of the world's best wines, and the Spanish tradition for guitar making has produced some of the world's best guitars, so the tradition within these areas of Andalucia has produced, and continues to produce, some of the finest Flamencos.

Since before the Bible was written, Andalucia was host to a great variety of civilisations including Carthaginians, Tartessos and Greeks, not to mention Phonecians, Romans (who named the peninsula Hisperia) and Visigoths, who have all left a physical trace on the landscape. It's likely they left other, less visible

---

[11]Joaquin Cortés and Dieguito El Cigala, for example
[12]See Chapter 5, "Who Sings Flamenco?"

influences, such as the way they moved their arms when they danced, or changed vocal pitch when they sang, or how they tuned their stringed instruments.[13] The intangible traces of past cultures probably hold the secrets which might otherwise reveal why Spain's southernmost region gave birth to such a compelling, unique culture.

Some flamenco forms come from the region of Murcia to the east of Andalucia which is called the *Levante*- literally The East. Known as the *Cantes de Levante* 'Songs from the East', or *cantes de las minas*- songs of the mines - they include the *cartagenera* named after Cartagena on the coast, and the *minera* and *taranta*. One of flamenco's most prestigious competitions is held in a mining town of Murcia each year, celebrating the mineras family of cantes with the prize of the *Lámpara Minera*-The Mining Lamp. Extremadura, to the North West of Andalucia bordering Portugal, isn't so well known as a flamenco region, it has produced a limited number of Flamencos whose families come from Badajoz, the capital of the province. Here, it is only the area of the Plaza Alta, which has traditionally been where Gypsies would meet during horse fairs, that has produced a few individual styles. Namely the *Tangos extremeños* and *jaleos* which very few *cabales*[14] can distinguish from any other *tangos* or bulerías rhythm. Porrinas de Badajoz (1924-1977) was the most famous cantaor from Extremadura, whose dynasty continues in the voice of his nephew Ramón El Portugués.

Many flamencos take their names from the place they come from: for example the guitarist Manolo *de Brenes*- from the town of Brenes just outside Seville; Antonio *Mairena,*- from Mairena del Alcor; Camarón *de La Isla,* from the Isla de San Fernando; El Chato *del La Isla,* also from San Fernando; Felix *de Utrera,* Fernanda and Bernarda *de Utrera* all from Utrera; Juan *El Lebrijano,*- from Lebrija; Manolo *Sanlúcar*-from Sanlúcar de Barrameda-; La Paquera *de Jerez* from Jerez; Porrinas *de Badajoz* from Badajoz the capital of Extremadura; Enrique *el Extremeño*; from Extremadura; Luis *de Córdoba*; Carmen *Linares*; La Perlita *de Huelva;* La Perla *de Cádiz*, La Niña *de La Puebla* from La Puebla de Cazalla; El Naranjito *de Triana* from the Seville neighbourhood of Triana, and so on. Many also take their artistic names from their parents, like Melchor *de Marchena* from Marchena, whose guitarist son calls himself Enrique *de Melchor;* or Ramón *de Algeciras* Paco de Lucía's brother who named himself after their home town Algeciras. Paco took his name from their mother: *de Lucía*. As a young performer with his brother Pepe de Lucía, they were known as Los Chiquitos *de Algeciras,* the kids from Algeciras.

GYPSY NEIGHBOURHOODS

It's quite likely the bands of Gypsies who reached Andalucia centuries ago and settled there, are the ancestors of today's traditional Gypsy neighbourhoods. Where Gypsies settled in large numbers, flamenco clans arose. In 1794 the Royal census noted that 126 *herreros*[15] lived in Triana alone, proving the neighbourhood has traditionally been home to Gypsies. The neighbourhoods known as Los Remedios and Triana in the city of Seville were traditionally Gypsy flamenco neighbourhoods until they were forced to resettle in outlying areas, which themselves have now become flamenco neighbourhoods. Such as the housing project known as *Las 3000 Viviendas*- (The 3000 Houses) the popular nick-name for the housing project south of Seville called the Polígano Sur where some of today's famous figures grew up, such as the Amador brothers, Rafael, Raimundo and Diego. Jerez is considered such a fundamentally flamenco city that many say at least one in ten of the population is either Gypsy or has Gypsy blood.

---

[13]The strings are the pieces of these ancient instruments which don't turn up in archeological digs; without them we can only guess how they sounded.
[14]In flamenco, this term refers to very specialized aficionados; more than just enthusiasts, they are experts.
[15]Metal workers, a traditionally Gypsy trade.

Gypsies settled in the villages around Seville such as Alcalá de Guadaira, Mairena del Alcor, Alcalá del Río and Morón de La Frontera all in the province of Seville. They spread out to Lebrija and Utrera, Marchena and La Puebla de Cazalla which are all traditionally flamenco villages. Places called 'De La Frontera'- of the frontier, are on the provincial borderline between Jerez and Sevilla and all share a flamenco history. Around Cádiz the areas of La Isla de San Fernando, El Puerto Real, El Puerto de Santa María, Sanlúcar de Barrameda and Cádiz itself are known as Los Puertos, which all claim distinct styles of *seguiriyas* and *soleares*.

The way of singing or the types of voices from each area are unique. The Seville flamenco style is usually called *Trianera* after the neighbourhood of Triana. The same sort of style is sung in the villages around it, like Mairena del Alcor, or Morón or Alcalá de Guadaira. The Jerez style influences Lebrija and Utrera, although these two small villages, halfway between Seville and Jerez have their own distinct flamenco feel. From Cádiz, a certain style developed based in the *cantiñas* family of palos- the *romeras, mirabras, caracoles, rosas* and *alegrías*- and most of the places around the port of Cádiz share the same influence, from Sanlúcar de Barrameda down to Chiclana. Huelva is known for its distinctive *fandangos de Huelva* and a great variety of local *fandangos*. Málaga is where the *malagueñas* style comes from, which is also musically related to the *fandangos*. The province of Cordoba has produced other famous and distinct local *fandangos*, like the *fandangos de Lucena* or the Cordoban version of *soleares* and *alegrías*. Linares in the province of Jaén used to be an important mining town and produced a specific *taranta*, the style always about mining. Almería produced the *tarantas* and later the *taranto*. In neighbouring Murcia where Andaluzes migrated to work in the mines of Cartagena and La Union, the *mineras* and *tarantas* developed with a local flavour which still distinguishes them.[16]

You can still hear these differences in the voices of professionals today, such as the voices of Fernanda and Bernarda de Utrera, or the Soto or Agujetas dynasties from Jerez- Vicente Soto Sordera or El Agujetas de Jerez- or the voice of La Paquera de Jerez. Or the Peñas from Lebrija- Juan Peña El Lebrijano- or Ines Bacan. El Chato de La Isla and Chano Lobato and Rancapino from Cádiz each have a style which is not only their own, but unique to the area they come from. The same thing goes for guitarists such as the Morao dynasty from Jerez, or the guitarists from Morón de La Frontera headed by the late Diego del Gastor (1908-1973). The Jerez school of guitar playing emphasises the thumb a lot, and the Morón style is quite simple and based on just a few flamenco techniques making it one of the most respected and *jondo* styles. In the past few years writers have begun to refer to a 'Barcelona' school of guitarists because of the success of Juan Manuel Cañizares and Chicuelo who both come from the capital of Catalonia. It's a bit early to distinguish a clear Barcelona style based on just these two artists. Cañizares uses a challenging jazz influenced style and often unusual tunings. Chicuelo has his own 'language' but shares some of these aspects. However, so does Antonio Carbonell *Montoyita* a Gypsy from Madrid who often accompanies Enrique Morente, proving such musical influences have little to do with geography.

---

[16]See Chapter 6, "What Are They Singing About?" - occupational hazards.

13

CHAPTER 2: FLAMENCO: A BIG PINK BIRD?

Flamenco is the Spanish word for a flamingo bird, and for the Belgian language which is almost identical to Dutch - Flemish. Why on earth does this music share the same name with such un-musical things? There are almost as many theories about the origins of the name for flamenco as there are saints and virgins in the Spanish calendar. The flamingo theory, one of the most absurd, has long been rejected. The idea was that the dancers looked like these long legged pink birds and so were named after them. The only interesting thing about this is that presumably he who dreamt it up, had seen flamingos. There's an accurate cave painting of a flamingo in Southern Spain which dates from around 5000 BC. so obviously this striking bird has been in Spanish territory for quite a while. Today there are populations of flamingos in parts of southern Spain as well as the Camargue region of southern France, from where they migrate to northern regions of Africa. The *phoenicopterus ruber* flamingo to you and me, was so named in 1758 and flamenco as we know it (the music, not the bird) started appearing around the same time, although not as a clearly defined style. Instead of asking whether flamenco was named after the bird why not ask if the bird is named after flamenco? Linnaeus chose the Latin name *Phoenicopteridae* for this family of birds because in ancient times flamingos were thought to be the descendent of the legendary Egyptian phoenix, which would rise anew from its ashes.

So if it's not named after the flamingo, how did it get its name?

FLAMENCO= FLEMISH SINGERS ?

The term flamenco was first used specifically in relation to the song and dance in 1853.[17] Up until then, it was used to refer to all sorts of things: a Gypsy, a contrabandist or petty criminal, a soldier, a style of dance, a style of dress, a type of knife, a carefree, irresponsible and burlesque nature ... even today it continues to serve as an umbrella term, since there really is no strict definition of 'Lo Flamenco'.

Hipólito Rossy who worked for the Spanish tax services -*Hacienda*- published his *Teoría del cante jondo* in 1966. His qualifications for such a book are that he studied music and regional folklore. With these qualifications he gave numerous talks about the basic musical structure of the flamenco forms and came up with the idea that because Flemish court musicians active in Spain during the Medieval ages performed music so well, other outstanding performers were said to be as good as the Flemish.[18] But this assumes an unimaginable association between the raw and sometimes bawdy song and dance style we know as flamenco, and stately court musicians whose interpretations were probably never witnessed by the majority of the ordinary population. This theory also assumes flamenco already consisted of a set of identifiable harmonic and rhythmic styles, as it does today, which presumably had no name before the Flemish court musicians turned up. It's a theory which also overlooks the minor detail of the gap of several hundred years between these Flemish cantors and the appearance of flamenco.

[17]*Silverio, Rey de los Cantaores.* J. Blas Vega Ed. La Posada, 1995.
[18]Hipólito Rossy, *Teoría del cante flamenco.*

FLAMENCO= GYPSY LANGUAGE?

Another theory states that the term Flamenco stems from the language which the Gypsies singing it used to speak among themselves... Flemish?

The original language spoken by Spanish Gypsies, which is no longer in use, is called *Caló*. It's generally accepted that the Gypsies in Southern Spain originated in the Punjab area of India and Pakistan. Caló is deemed to come from the original Hindi and Punjabi word for 'black'- *kala*. Gypsies often refer to themselves as *calé,* and *La Gente del Bronze-* The Dark Skinned Ones. The original bands of Gypsies may have come from the territories between Afghanistan and India where the dialect spoken is Pushtu, which shares some of its vocabulary with Caló. The word *jerga,* or *jirga* in these lands means a gathering, usually a 'sitting' of village elders, which is a traditional way of discussing and planning community matters. The term became familiar to the West during the American bombing of Afghanistan in late 2001, when the international community began planning the benighted country's future and calling for a *Loya Jirga;* a parliamentary debate among the country's leaders.

Jerga is the Spanish term for *argot* or slang and is supposedly derived from *jerigonza* meaning a difficult language to understand. *Jerigonza* may stem from the Provençal word *gergons.* Provençal was widely used in Spain throughout the Middle ages and a few words left over from this period still remain. But jerga may also have entered Spanish via the Caló language. It would not be the only originally Gypsy word in circulation even today.[19] *Jerga* may also be the origin of the word *juerga* which is an Andalucian -and specifically flamenco term -for a riotous, boozy party. The dictionary of the Real Academia de La Lengua gives the origin of *juerga* as *huelga* which means 'a strike'- as in stopping work in protest. The esteemed academics' reasons for giving this origin seem more to do with the stereotypical image of the lazy Andalucian, (whose pronunciation of *huelga* would indeed sound more like *huerga,*) than with etymological study. Andalucia does have a long history of social strife, but common sense makes it hard to believe that every time a worker's cooperative downed tools, they simply threw a song and dance.

Jerigonza or *jerga* is also the term used for the special language of certain trades; the jargon of the trade. Most groups of enthusiasts use a type of slang language, a jargon peculiar to their *afición*. By using an argot, such groups establish a separate identity for themselves, reinforcing their sense of belonging to an exclusive club. Look at computer buffs or the art world, where people sometimes use ordinary words in an extraordinary way to differentiate themselves from those who are not 'in the know'. This is also true in flamenco and bullfighting, where the terms often overlap from one *afición* to another, since both arts developed during the same period.

In the 1700s in Spain the words *jerga* and *germanía* (spelt using either a 'g' or a 'j') were both used to define a slang spoken by a certain group of people, usually petty criminals. As Gypsies were thought of as petty criminals, the language they spoke amongst themselves was said to be *germanía. Germanía* was therefore the term for Caló, although Caló was a language and not simply a jargon. A small publication recording prison life in Seville in the 18th Century,[20] describes how prisoners at night would sing to their women folk using guitars or harps to accompany themselves while they sang their *cantares jermanes.*[21] Gradually the term *germanía* has come to be applied to any language the Spanish don't understand, so Caló, Flemish or Dutch,

[19] See Chapter 7, "The European Gypsies" and "What's The Gypsy's Story?"
[20] A. Zoido, 'La Prisión General', Ediciones Porrua 2000.
[21] Ibid.

15

German and English were all bunched together and called *germanía*. Since the Gypsies were said to speak in *germanía* and Flemish is also *germanía*, so the theory arose which said the art is named after the language they spoke: *Flamenco=Flemish=foreign language.* Perhaps one of the most convoluted theories about the term!

[*Germanía* shouldn't be confused with *germán* which has the same use in Spanish as it does in English, that is, it refers to a German- a person from Germany! To this day, countries which use the German language - *Alemán* in Spanish- are referred to as *países de habla germánica*.]

FLAMENCO = A SOLDIER FROM FLANDERS?

A more plausible theory relies on the tendency communities have of turning a word's meaning around entirely. Like today's fashion for saying something which is really good, is 'bad'. Gypsies knew the negative connotations of the word 'Gypsy', and did their best to improve their standing in their communities. In the 1700s it was almost an insult to call someone a butcher, coach driver or metal worker, because these jobs were predominantly held by Gypsies. It was an insult to call someone a Gypsy then, just as it is still today. My aunt uses the term Flamenco and Gypsy interchangeably, and both as an insult. To be a Gypsy often meant imprisonment and those who worked in these jobs went out of their way to deny they had any Gypsy blood in them. They formed brotherhoods, and formally declared themselves to be baptised and inscribed in their local parish, which was a requirement of many of the anti-Gypsy laws.[22]

In 1602 several Gypsy families who had been serving the Spanish rulers in Flanders, returned to Spain with unique identity papers granting them official dispensation to live wherever they chose, and take up any jobs they chose. Because these Gypsies had been in Flanders for about 24 years, they were referred to as 'Flamencos'- the Spanish word for Flemish- when they came home. This also distinguished them from the ordinary *gitano*, who was not allowed to live where he pleased or work at what he pleased. There is evidence of the 'Flemish' Gypsy families brandishing their official dispensations to explain that they were exempt from the official laws condemning Gypsies to particular trades and neighbourhoods, and that they settled in Andalucia over the course of the 18th century. Although it's unlikely these Gypsies returned from the Netherlands singing and dancing flamenco, other Gypsies would have seen how differently they were treated and may have started calling themselves Flamencos to see if they could get away with it. So by association, the term may have been used at first jokingly, since Gypsies clearly have nothing in common with northern Europeans, and then earnestly by Gypsies themselves in the hope of improving their living conditions. When these same Gypsies began playing and singing and dancing flamenco in public, gradually their style of music became known as flamenco and so the term was also mixed up with being a Gypsy.

Whether this theory is true or not, Flamenco became synonymous with Gypsy and the words to some of the cantes reflect this:

Flamenquita que dirías	Flamenco lady what would you say
si yo hiciera contigo	If I did the same bad things to you
Esas malas partías?	That you do to me?

---

[22]Ibid.

FLAMENCO= ESCAPED MOOR?

The challenge to explain the semantic origin of the word, produced another theory linking it with Arabic which is still reproduced in places which should know better, or at least have done some research. The idea linked two words *fela* and *mengu*. The first word is from the Arabic *fellah* which originally meant a peasant. The second word was supposed to mean 'runaway' or 'escaped'. Since flamenco was believed originally to have ties with banditry, this explanation fit the bill for many people, who also ignored the fact that flamenco didn't exist during the time of the Moorish occupation.[23] In Felix Grande's "Memoria del Flamenco"[24] he wrote of his discussions with an Arabic speaking friend and poet, and their attempts to resolve this debate. They found the second word simply doesn't exist in Arabic, which you have to admit, makes an Arabic philological origin for flamenco rather doubtful.

FLAMENCO= HORSE KNIFE?

Felix Grande also said that the term may come from the name given to a particular style of knife which Gypsies used to arm themselves with, similar to the Sihks of India, for whom the knife is an intrinsic element of their religious identity.[25] When the prisoners in Seville's jails sang through the railings to their loved ones, they used knives to beat the rhythm on the iron window grates. Gypsy horse traders carried a special knife which adds credibility to Felix Grande's idea. Throughout the history of Gypsy culture, certain occupations have traditionally been pursued; sheep shearing and horse or donkey clipping and trading, among them. In 1997 I read an article in *El País* newspaper which reinforced this theory of a link between the name of a knife, and the name of a style of music. Funnily enough, it was a report on the beatification of a Gypsy.

In 1936, Ceferino Giménez Malla, a Gypsy who happened to be a devout Christian, was executed by a republican firing squad in the city of Barbastro, in the province of Aragón. His crime was not his ethnicity, but that of having defended a priest by brandishing his knife against attack from a group of republican soldiers. Ceferino was arrested because he refused to give up his rosary, (not because he was carrying a knife) and subsequently executed with the horribly careless barbarity which accompanies all wars.

Like the famous Andalucian poet García Lorca, Ceferino's execution was not officially decreed, but happened basically because he was in the wrong place at the wrong time. Unlike García Lorca, Ceferino Giménez Malla (another spelling for this name is Maya- a common Flamenco Gypsy name) was beatified in 1997[26], because he gave his life rather than give up his faith. But this story is of interest to flamenco because it brings to light the fact that the knife Ceferino carried was a *fleme*, a style of knife used specifically for bleeding horses. The name *fleme* stems from the Provençal word *flecme*.

The Gypsies of Spain are said to have entered the country from France in the 15th Century via the Pyrenees, the Provençe region where Provençal is still spoken by a minority. There have always been Spanish Gypsy populations in Catalunya and Southern France, (where the Gypsy Kings come from) and therefore, always some links with flamenco in these regions. Is it not possible that the name of this knife, so common among the Gypsy horse traders, long ago became associated with those who carried it and who knew how to use it? The ending *enco* as used in 'flamenco' is used in argot or *germanía* to describe those who come from a specific place, or something which looks like or is similar to the word it's added to. People from Ibiza for

---

[23]At least, not as we know it.
[24]Espasa Calpe, 1987.
[25]Since Spain's Gypsies originated from the same region as the Sihks, it's possible that the Gypsy habit of carrying a knife goes back to the same historical period.
[26]The CD *Un Gitano de Ley* (Nuevos Medios 1997) was recorded in celebration of his beatification.

example, are *Ibicencos*. Thus, he who carried a 'fleme' may have been referred to as a *flemenco* and the pronunciation of this gradually evolved into *flamenco*. Although it's not common in today's Spanish, *enco* is sometimes added to a word to make it an insult. Which also tarries with the fact that the terms Gypsy and Flamenco were used interchangeably to describe criminals, ruffians and 'undesirables' in past centuries. And anybody with anything to do with them, such as horse traders or knife-carriers- *flemencos* would be disrespected.

Since the music and dance style we know today wasn't called flamenco until the 1800s, it's obvious the meaning of the name itself has undergone as many changes as the art itself. Just as finding a definition of flamenco is almost impossible, so finding a definitive explanation for the name seems equally impossible. Which adds to the aura of mystery and enigma that surrounds it, and the people who perform it.

CHAPTER 3: HOW DEEP IS DEEP?

WHAT IS CANTE JONDO?

"Good singing hurts; it doesn't make you happy, it hurts."[27]

Flamenco contains a great range of emotions, from the light hearted and purely joyous and bawdy, to the more dignifying emotions of loss, sorrow, grief and injustice. But just as depression is more complex, more interesting than joy, so the flamenco forms which embody the darker side of life, are thought of as the most important *palos*, by which everything else must be measured. *El cante jondo*, in flamenco dialect literally "deep song"- is considered the oldest style of flamenco singing. The name comes from the Andaluz pronunciation of the Spanish for 'deep'; *hondo*, which becomes *jondo*. It's called Deep Song because it involves the deepest emotions. For purists, el cante jondo is the only definition of flamenco, but that would mean other types of performance are less flamenco, or are something else entirely. Early on in flamenco's history, a distinction was made between 'flamenco' and 'cante jondo'. Flamenco was all those styles which were thought to have developed from local folk songs, like the *fandangos* family, and *el cante jondo* meant those styles thought to be purely Gypsy. Only the *seguiriyas* and *soleares,* the *toná* and *tientos* were considered *cante jondo,* also called *cante puro,* or *cante gitano.*

A cantaor singing one of these cantes must have a profound knowledge of them because they're the most demanding stylistically and emotionally. He should know all the regional stylistic variations, like the Seguiriyas de Triana (from the neighbourhood of Triana in Seville) Seguiriyas de Jerez or de Cádiz, or the Seguiriyas de Los Puertos- from the Puerto de Santa María in Cádiz for example, and also the different personal interpretations which have been passed on from one generation to the next; for example the Seguiriyas de Chacón or the Seguiriyas de El Loco Mateo. Often the differences between these regional variations are minimal, a difference in the melody or even something more basic, simply the different subjects. A cantaor who sings cante jondo is expected to produce a *cante rancio* -meaning 'mature', like a well-aged wine- with traditional themes, and filled with the characteristics valued by aficionados such as emotional expressivity above clarity, or even being in tune. In all of the *cantes jondos* the singer 'complains' and almost sobs his woes.

"In the voice, the fundamental thing is feeling, an ability to express that foundation of pain there is in flamenco. I think that flamenco is above all a sad song."[28]

But the basic emotional character of a *cante jondo,* that it deeply moves both the singer and the audience can be applied to almost all the flamenco cantes. For example a bulerías, malagueña or a taranto can also be called jondo if they're delivered with moving sincerity.

WHAT IS FLAMENCO PURO?

In 1926 the Malagueño (from Málaga) José Carlos de Luna published "De Cante Grande y Cante Chico" - "All About Great Song and Small Song"- which led to the separation of flamenco styles into groups of 'great' styles and 'small'- with the 'small' forms supposedly light-hearted and easy to perform. The implication is that the 'small' forms are less artistically valid and less worthy of attention. This distinction doesn't really exist. As the poet Manuel Machado said: "Flamenco is to love and live, to understand and smile, at this

---

[27]This was the definition Juan Talegas (1887-1971) gave of the effect of hearing Manuel Torre (1878-1923), legendary Gypsy singer.
[28]Camarón de la Isla, *El Europeo* magazine N°33, June 1991.

and that, and something which is beyond." Flamencologists latched onto the distinction of some forms as 'great' and others 'small', and some forms 'pure' and others not, but these are just labels, still used by some despite the fact that what's great or small is a personal choice, and ultimately depends on the quality of the interpretation. Most artists within flamenco are now publicly discrediting this sort of labelling.

CANTE JONDO, CANTE GITANO

Cante jondo, or as it's also called *cante gitano* was believed to have emerged from the secretive Gypsy community and is considered to be the "real thing": pure flamenco, *El Cante Puro*. This theory has been handed down since the cantaor Antonio Mairena and poet Ricardo Molina wrote Mundo Y Formas del Cante Flamenco[29] where they published their ideas on the origins of flamenco.[30] For Mairena, who established his beliefs with such conviction that they are still repeated and taken as gospel, el cante puro could only be sung by a Gypsy. The interpretation of cante puro boils down to a more primitive style of delivery, just the singer baring his soul and the guitarist accompanying him. The purity of delivery, or purity of emotions might be the best definition.

When asked, "What is purity?" Camarón replied: *"Try to keep the primitive element of el cante, know how to stay un-tamed. For example, I know I'm already quite refined, although I fight to preserve the purity.... To be pure is to try to conserve oneself, not to change with the years."*[31]

For many older aficionados today, it seems only singers from the past knew what *el cante puro* was, and they consider that all the new tunings and chords in recent flamenco have killed this off. This reminds me of the saying among classical music fans that, "The best conductors are the dead ones," meaning–nobody plays it like they did anymore. Flamenco must naturally lose some of its original force as the social conditions which existed while it was developing are disappearing. Today's singers simply don't suffer the same disadvantages their ancestors did, their environment is easier to survive, there is no shortage of food and nobody travels on a donkey's back anymore to get to the next village's flamenco festival to earn a few hundred pesetas.

The nostalgia for the old days and the old ways of flamenco is very similar to the movement within classical music to return to the past, to perform music on the original instruments of the composer's day and to get ever closer to the *authentic* sound and interpretation of the composer's music. This movement exists among those who completely ignore the fact that what is *authentic* is relative. Relative to everything we've heard in between times, and everything we've lived. As the famous Russian classical pianist Anatoli Ugorski said:

"You can go to a shop and buy an authentic leather coat, but you can't ask for an authentic Bach; we'd have to resuscitate him. In our vision and interpretation of Bach today we have to take into account the 300 years of history which separates us from him. Surely, to go to a concert of so-called authentic interpretation you shouldn't listen in modern concert halls, or even dress the way we do, let alone arrive by car or by plane...?"[32]

---

[29]First published in 1963.
[30]See Chapter 7, "What's the Gypsy's Story?"
[31]Camarón de La Isla, *El Europeo* magazine, N° 33, June 1999.
[32]*El País* Friday October 13th 2000, Interview by J. Ruiz Mantilla.

CHAPTER 4: WHO INVENTED FLAMENCO?

Nobody ever sat down in a bar one evening in Andalucia and said: "Right, we want to create a new style of music, and we're going to call it flamenco." It simply evolved naturally from the continuous evolution which *is* popular music and entertainment. Perhaps the closest we can get to defining who is fundamentally responsible for flamenco music and dance as we know it today, is to say that it was invented in Andalucia, by Andalucians. Together, both Andalucian Gypsies and non-Gypsies gradually created a distinct style of song and dance, out of traditional folk music and verses already in existence. But just as not every American plays jazz every day, neither does every Andalucian sing, dance or play flamenco. Nor do they listen to it continually, nor many of them recognise the forms.

Everybody associates flamenco with the Gypsies of Spain. Only the Spanish Gypsies, but not all of them, sing and dance flamenco. But non-Gypsies in Andalucia and elsewhere - whom the Gypsies call *payos* or sometimes *gachós* - also perform flamenco in the same way. However, since Gypsies have been settled in Spain since the 1400s and flamenco only developed in the late 1700s, it can't be attributed to them alone. Gypsies in other parts of Europe share the same origins as the Andaluz *Gitano*. How come none of them play flamenco? If it were a purely Gypsy invention, surely they would also be performing it. We can't say the Moors of Spain invented it either, since the almost 800 years of their rule have left no mention of flamenco. As no solid evidence about who invented flamenco was available, just about anybody could create a persuasive theory and become an authority. As the Spanish saying goes: 'In the land of the blind, the one-eyed man is King.' Gypsies have no reasonable explanation for the emergence of flamenco (on the rare occasion when they're asked) other than to say that they learned the *cantes* from their ancestors. Since their history is as confused and obscure to them as it is to the rest of us, the origins of Gypsy Flamenco remain a mystery.

WHAT A PAIN

To point a finger at one particular ethnic group and claim they invented flamenco, has led to a great confusion. It's best to remember that when flamenco was first written about, it was not the tidy defined selection of styles we recognise today. It was an emerging art: in development, it wasn't born fully formed! Because of all the words about suffering in *el cante flamenco* people have tried to attribute it to each different ethnic group that has suffered throughout Spain's history: Spanish Gypsies, Spanish-Arabs, and Sefardic Jews. *Pena*-"suffering" in Spanish- is a recurring theme, an ancestral pain who's cause nobody has been able to explain convincingly. All kinds of colourful theories have been published trying to explain it. It's traditionally thought that Gypsies 'invented' flamenco, since this *pena* is their history and experience. It's only in recent times that the full extent of the persecution of Gypsies has been fully investigated.[33] The Andalucian Gypsy originated in the Punjab area of northern India and present-day Pakistan, so their *pena* was sometimes said to be because of their exile from their ancestral home, hundreds of years ago. Those who tried to explain the origins of flamenco as Arabic, attributed the recurring theme of *pena* to the expulsion of the Moors from Granada. The musicologist Christian Poché[34] describes Arabic-Andaluz music- a particular style of music which developed in the Arab ruled regions of Spain- as one long ode to absence; the lament of the homesick Moor living in *Al-Andalus* - mainland Spain, far from his homeland. Today that homeland would be the areas of Algeria, Tunisia

---

[33]See Chapter 7, "What's the Gypsy's Story?"
[34]*La Música Arabigo-Andaluza*, Ediciones Akal 1997

and Morocco. Those who trace flamenco's origins back to the Sefardic Jews suppose the *pena* comes from their forced conversion to Christianity, and their expulsion from Spain under the Catholic monarchs. But besides the vast gaps in time between all these historic events and the emergence of flamenco in the 1780s, all these explanations assume that the indigenous Andalucians, for some unknown reason, adopted these people's pain and suffering as their own, since the indigenous Andaluz also performs flamenco.

Since flamenco has evolved from so many different influences, socio-cultural and musical, and continues to evolve and absorb, it's not possible to say Gypsies invented it, or it was the Moors, or Jews or Greeks, Phonecians or Carthaginians, Pakistanis or Egyptians, who first sang and danced flamenco, because it has a little bit of influence from each one of these cultures. Flamenco did not arrive on the scene as a ready formed set of dances and songs. Those that we see and hear today are the result of years of practice, assimilation, and interpretation by artists, some with more creative talent than others.

If the Arabs or Sefardic Jews had been the creators of flamenco as it emerged in the 1800s, why are they not performing it today? The Moors who were finally driven out of Christian Spain in the late 1500s, took their customs and their distinct Arabic-andaluz music with them to Morocco, Algeria, Tunisia, and even as far as Tripoli in Libya and Aleppo in Syria. Obviously the ingredients necessary for flamenco were not to be found in these places since flamenco did not develop here.

The fact that some palos under the flamenco umbrella have definite folkloric roots -evident in the words, harmonies and the rhythms- shows that some flamenco is the result of adapting existing folk music and song to a peculiar *flamenco* interpretation, which probably does have its roots in a primitive style of Gypsy cante. When you see Agujetas de Jerez gush out a stream of emotion, or El Capullo de Jerez singing out of tune, and seemingly oblivious to the strict rhythmic form the guitarist is adhering to, it appears you're seeing something close to the roots of Gypsy cante. When you see the non-Gypsies José Menese or Enrique Morente performing, you're seeing the *payo* adapting his ways to the Gypsy's more spontaneous style, giving it thought and structure. Non-Gypsy performers seem to think before they sing, whereas the Gypsy's style always seems more immediate and instinctive.

FLAMENCO'S FOUNDING FATHERS

There are several legendary figures who more and more, are being credited with laying the foundations of flamenco as we know it today. Artists such as Don Antonio Chacón (1869- 1929) Manuel Torres (1878-1933) and Pastora Pavón 'La Niña De Los Peines' (Sevilla 1890-1969) are increasingly presented as the founding fathers of flamenco cante. Before the advent of recording, before flamenco was even called flamenco, there were artists performing professionally who influenced these legendary figures. Perhaps the most important of these was Silverio Franconetti (1823-1889) who was known during his lifetime as *El Rey de los Cantaores Andaluzes*- The King of Andalucian Singing-.[35] José Luis Ortiz Nuevo has come to the conclusion that:

"With some certainty we can say that the art of flamenco as we know it today was formulated as a unique aesthetic in the last third of the 19th Century, in the Café Cantantes and thanks to the work of creation, classification, presentation and synthesis of an exceptional musician, the Sevillian Silverio Franconetti."[36]

Some of the figures most frequently quoted in lists of forefathers may not belong there. Tomás El Nitri, for example who is best known for being the recipient of the first *Llave de Oro del Cante*- The Golden Key of El Cante- who is said to have refused to sing for Silverio. El Nitri had a very limited repertoire and never sang

---

[35]*Silverio, Rey de los Cantaores.* J. Blas Vega, Ediciones la Posada 1995.
[36]Idem.

professionally, only singing at family gatherings, or for friends and rich Gypsies. The award seems to have been made by a group of admirers and had absolutely no repercussions, it was not even reported in the press of the day and neither was El Nitri! It would appear he was one of the many non-professional Gypsy cantaores who may have had a special way of singing one or two styles which influenced the few who heard him. Many of the Gypsy artists born in the early 1900s recall members of their family who sang or danced with exceptional *flamencura*[37] which seems to uphold Demófilo's and Mairena's[38] belief that flamenco began behind closed doors, in the privacy of Gypsy homes. Not all of those who sang and danced flamenco during the late 1800s and early 1900s was a professional with a school or following of disciples, and not all of those artists whose names have come down to us in print or through recollections and anecdotes deserve the importance bestowed on them.

CREATIONISTS AND RE-CREATIONISTS

The guitarist Luís Maravilla (b. Seville 1914) is one of the few who can recall the historic figure of Chacón, a non-Gypsy credited with up grading flamenco's image from the whore houses and drunken bars it was associated with, by always appearing neatly dressed in a suit and behaving impeccably with an air of dignity usually associated with respectable classical musicians. In 1927 the young Luís Maravilla was asked to accompany the great Chacón in a party organised by the Duke of Medinaceli. Later on when he worked at the famous Villa Rosa flamenco club, he recalled:

> *Chacón was considered by everybody to be the greatest cantaor of the age (...) In those days everybody admired him. I don't recall ever having heard anybody criticise him as an artist. Later on yes, but that's more recent, people who never knew him. In those days, there was an excellent relationship between Gypsies and payos. I never saw a Gypsy discriminating or vice versa. Juanito Mojama, one of the Gypsies I've spent most time with, admired Chacón and imitated him in his cante and everything. He always wore black with a white shirt, he learned that from Chacón, and his sisters would press his pants and wash his shirt daily. He was always as smart as a pin. So much so that the Duke of Andria once said to him, "Juanito! You're cleaner than me!"*[39]

Chacón is said to have given several cantes their defining form, cantes which existed before him but which lacked the defined musical and melodic structure he gave them. Today they are well established in the repertory: the *caracoles*, a cante with the compás of soleares, the *granaína* a member of the fandangos family, the *malagueña,* of which he is credited with developing six different styles, and the *tientos*, a slow tangos. La Niña de Los Peines, who worked during the same period as Chacón and Torres, is credited with the 'creation' of the *bamberas*, sung to the compás of a soleá. The words to the *bamberas* are ancient, and La Niña simply adapted them to a flamenco compás and style of delivery but with such personal artistry that they became accepted into the fold of the flamenco stylistic family. As so often in flamenco, the cante existed before the artist, but the personality of the artist was such that the cante gained distinction and musicality and ended up accepted as fundamentally flamenco. Manuel Torres is most often remembered for his interpretation of seguiriyas[40] and bulerías, the emblematic style from his home town, Jerez.

---

[37]See Chapter 5, "Flamenco Generations."
[38]See Chapter 9, The Gospel According to..." and "What's The History?
[39]*Luis Maravilla: Por Derecho:* Miguel Espín, J.M. Gamboa 1990.
[40]See Chapter 6-"What's in a Seguiriyas?"

The flamencologist Pedro Camacho said that Manuel Torres "modernized the *seguiriya* to make it a contemporary song, less rough, more emotional and familiar to the Andalucian, thereby becoming the prototype for all who followed him."[41] Which begs the question: How rough and unfamiliar to the Andalucian could this difficult style be? From the digitally cleaned up samples of his art[42] we can hear the proof supporting the legend surrounding him. His sound and inspired delivery really does cut you like a knife, as Fernando El de Triana declared: "His sound gets in your ears and doesn't leave you." Torres was renowned for his irregularity in performance, like today's Agujetas de Jerez he could sometimes turn up and sing masterfully and other times barely croak a line acceptably, as this memoir recalls:

> *Midnight. We had just entered the room. Ignacio Sánchez Mejías and a couple of his French friends were there, Manuel Torres, another dancer and a guitarist. We were going to hear the famous gypsy Manuel Torres. Throughout dinner, Ignacio, a great admirer of his, had spoken to us of his art: 'It's something so moving. It's unique. You hear him sing a seguiriyas and then dying is not important to you anymore. One cannot find in the world anything so beautiful as to equal Manuel Torres' singing.' Torres sat himself in a corner and began drinking wine, silent, as though he weren't there. The other singer sang. The dancer danced. Manuel Torres didn't look at the dance nor listen to the singing. Ignacio tells us: 'You have to leave him be. He's a pure gypsy.' Three o'clock in the morning. Manuel Torres drinks his thirty glasses of liquor. He starts ... to sing? No, to talk. Until five in the morning he was talking about greyhounds non-stop. The French fell asleep, completely drunk. Daylight broke. Under my breath I asked Sanchez Mejías, "Do you think he'll sing?" And he replied, very contrite, "I'm afraid not. When he gets going on his greyhounds, he may not sing until two in the afternoon. I was shocked. But are we staying here until two in the afternoon?" Ignacio, completely normal replied: "Ah, of course! You don't know what a seguiriya sung by this man is like." I knew precisely, at nine thirty in the morning. Ignacio Sanchez Mejías, that most masculine of men, cried. I had goose bumps. My nerves shook with the most intense of emotions. It has been many years. Nobody gave me as deep an emotion as the seguiriyas sung by Manuel Torres.*[43]

Torres was known as a difficult character, more interested in his hunting dogs and fighting cocks than giving a good performance. As one of the invited guests at the 1922 Concurso de Cante Jondo in Granada, he shared a hotel with Andrés Segovia the classical guitarist who served on the jury. The constant crowing coming from Manuel Torres' room where he had stashed one of his fighting cocks in a wardrobe caused Segovia to complain.

From the documentary records we have of these singers it's safe to say they were not so much creators or inventors as they were defining interpreters. All of the styles they are individually associated with had been sung before them by other masters, about whom we know much less, and whose birth dates and biographies are barely known. As flamenco is such a relatively young art, we are fortunate that much of its history has actually been caught in recorded sound, which we have the technology today to enhance and reproduce on CD. The danger with this is that flamencologists begin to credit only those artists who managed to leave behind an audible record as being responsible for its foundation and 'invention.' The opposite is also dangerous: crediting figures whose names keep cropping up, pre-sound recording, as being the only ones who really knew the styles in an unadulterated and pure state.

[41]Blas Vega, notes for *Manuel Torres, La Leyenda del Cante*; Sonifolk CD 20146
[42]Manuel Torres, *La Leyenda del Cante 1909-1930*, Sonifolk 20146
[43]Idem.

CHAPTER 5: WHO SINGS FLAMENCO?

Federico García Lorca, the famous poet from Granada, declared that Manuel Torre (1878-1933) the Gypsy *cantaor* had: "more culture in his veins than any ordinary Spaniard." This offended a lot of middle class Spaniards who thought of Gypsies as illiterate, uneducated, and untrustworthy. In a word-*uncultured.* Flamenco is originally the art of the peasant and illiterate, and that's why it's rejected by many Spaniards who are offended that such a 'low brow' art form has come to represent the whole country. Even today, most Flamencos come from humble backgrounds and there are still performers who can't read or write well. There are few rich Flamencos, and few from middle or upper class origins. Antonio Ranchal is an unusual exception who specialised in the fandangos of Lucena. He was actually from an aristocratic family and was well known during the 1960s as one of the best interpreters of these fandangos.

Those who perform flamenco come from families where it has always been a backdrop, or have grown up in neighbourhoods surrounded by it. But this isn't a hard and fast rule either. Many of today's professional performers came to flamenco through some kind of organic progression; a dancer may begin with classical training but more readily identify with flamenco, and some guitarists have taken a similar route. Performers such as the sax and flute player Jorge Pardo or the percussionist Tino Di Geraldo have come from classical and jazz backgrounds but they've been able to integrate these elements into modern flamenco.

VIVA SANTIAGO

In Jerez, there are two Gypsy neighbourhoods regarded as profoundly flamenco; La Plazuela, and the *barrios*[44] around the churches of San Miguel and Santiago which have produced several dynasties of artists who have become legends. Watching volume 6 of *Rito Geografía del Toque*, you'll see the guitarist Manuel Morao performing a seguiriyas next to an old lady: Tia Añica La Piriñaca. As he begins playing, she swipes a handkerchief across her face several times, suffering under the hot glare of the camera lights. But soon she becomes absorbed by his playing and when he ends she cries: "Viva Santiago!" in reference to the neighbourhood where they were both born and raised. Some say one in every four *Jerezanos* has Gypsy blood in him, such was the size of the Gypsy population who all danced and sang. According to Tía Añica almost everyone in Jerez knows how to do something within flamenco: "*It was rare to find a house in which they didn't know how to sing or dance.*" In Cádiz the neighbourhood of Santa María is traditionally flamenco, and Flamencos from Sevilla are most proud of their neighbourhood of Triana, which was originally the Gypsy quarter.

Although many of today's professionals are non-Gypsies who don't come from traditional flamenco families nor even from Andalucia (like Mayte Martin or Miguel Poveda, both from Barcelona) it's still generally true that in order to sing flamenco, you have to be born into it. There are no *cantaores* or *cantaoras* who came to flamenco after a classical vocal training. A few decide to leave *el cante* and go into pop and Spanish *folk-canción*, such as Rocío Jurado and Isabel Pantoja, or her cousin Chiquetete for example, who have all become superstars singing in the 'aflamencada' style of dramatic *coplas* which are closely related to flamenco. Chiquetete is from a family of Flamencos, and his departure from an early career in flamenco was sadly mourned when he decided to take the more commercial route. Paco de Lucía's brother Pepe de Lucía, has one of the best flamenco voices of his generation and one of the most extensive repertoires in flamenco. He's what's known as a *cantaor largo*, which means he knows all the different versions of cantes and sings all the styles well- yet he chooses to compose and perform a more pop-flamenco-ballad style. Those who have made

[44]neighbourhoods

a living out of the *copla andaluza* such as Isabel Pantoja or Rocío Jurado are sometimes called *folkloricas* and this is one reason why most people in flamenco don't like to class flamenco as a folk form. *Folkloric* isn't a term used to specify high art or good quality in Spain, but sometimes the word is used to criticize something for its simplicity and common popularity.

GYPSY'S MEMORIES

Today, flamencologists who credit Gypsies with the origins of flamenco abide by Mairena's declaration that it used to be sung only in private, and that it went through a so-called 'hermetic phase' (also known as a 'pre-flamenco' phase) before it emerged into the cafés and theatres of the mid 1800s. According to Mairena, before flamenco became professionalised it was exclusively Gypsy and he called it *cante gitano*. For him, *flamenco* or *cante andaluz* was no longer authentically Gypsy. Some doubt this pre-flamenco time existed, however, since it coincides historically with the time when Gypsies were very well integrated in their communities. Silverio Franconetti (1823-1889) was the first cantaor to be profiled in a biography written in 1881 by the folklorist Manuel Machado y Álvarez *Demófilo*. From Franconetti's professional activity we can trace a little of the early history of the cantes, which Mairena would have us believe were only sung initially by Gypsies. This means that Silverio- who was not a Gypsy- had to learn from the Gypsies and so must have been able to mingle with them, and, that they must have shared their secrets with him. How hermetic and secretive is that? Perhaps because of these contradictions- that Silverio must have learned from the Gypsies yet the Gypsies were keeping things to themselves–Mairena and Molina declared that Silverio deformed the cantes and sweetened them, robbing them of their original force. Nevermind the fact that neither of them had ever heard Silverio sing.

From the Gypsies themselves come the memories which confirm the roots of flamenco in their ancestors. Juan Talegas, born in 1891, talked of his grandfather being a better singer than his better known uncle Joaquin de La Paula. If singers from the turn of the 19th Century could remember how their grandfathers sang and learned from them, it seems logical to assume those grandfathers would also have learned from their grandfathers. This takes us back several generations into the mid-1800s, even allowing for the fact that early marriage within Gypsy communities means most grandparents are only in their 40s! Most Gypsies talk of uncles and aunts and grandfathers and grandmothers who weren't 'professionals' but who excelled in some style or other, usually *soleares*, *seguiriyas* and *tangos* which are often called the original *cante gitano*.

There's a branch of modern flamenco which still embraces this non-commercial aspect. Flamenco sung in small private clubs, *peñas* and during family gatherings is perhaps as close as we can get today to *flamenco puro*. For most serious aficionados, flamenco can't be considered an entertainment, it's more of a catalyst or ritual. This means flamenco used to be very different from what we see in festivals, concert halls and theatres today. It has evolved over the past 200 years, digesting many musical influences like traditional religious songs, local folk songs and dances and some not so local (the *alegrías* is supposed to be influenced by the jota from Aragón in the north) and rhythms and movements from Latin America and Africa.

There are two basic styles of flamenco interpretation, the Gypsy's and the non-Gypsy's or *payos*. Historic *payo* cantaores such as Don Antonio Chacón, Pepe Marchena, José Cepero, or stars of today like Enrique Morente, Carmen Linares or José Menese all sing with their heads as well as their hearts. Their style is different from that of such Gypsies as Agujetas, Manuel Torre, Terremoto, La Paquera de Jerez, Fernanda and Bernarda de Utrera, or Camarón de la Isla whose styles are less refined and thought out, less rehearsed or practiced, and more instinctive. The differences are very subtle and almost impossible to define, but once you've listened to a lot of flamenco, your flamenco intuition will start to show you the differences. Famous figures in flamenco's past are both *payos* and *gitanos*, in almost equal measure. Most are from Andalucía, Extremadura or Murcia, and a significant few from Catalunya, most of whom originated in Andalucia or of Andalucian parentage. The vast majority are from underprivileged, humble backgrounds. Within flamenco (and Spain generally), it's not frowned upon to make racial distinctions between the Gypsy and non-Gypsy and most will agree that Gypsy flamencos have a certain edge over their *payo* counterparts, an indefinable special- ness that guarantees their interpretations will raise the hairs on the back of your head.

Among today's big names, the best known non-Gypsies are the guitarists Paco de Lucía, Manolo Sanlúcar and Vicente Amigo; the controversial *cantaor* Enrique Morente, Carmen Linares and the orthodox José Menese; and *bailaoras* María Pages, Eva la Yerbabuena and Sara Baras – all *payos,* along with the *bailaores* Javier Baron and Antonio Canales. Gypsies and *payos* exist within flamenco side by side, often forming exceptional partnerships, and it's always been this way. Antonio Chacón, one of the most important figures in flamenco's history was a non-Gypsy; he formed a partnership with the Gypsy guitarist Ramón Montoya which became legendary. The late Camarón de la Isla and his last accompanist Tomatito were both Gypsies, but Camarón's fame was founded alongside his non-Gypsy *compadre* (colleague) Paco de Lucía.

FLAMENCO GENERATIONS

Antonio Mairena (1909-1983) recounted that, *"My mother Aurora danced the tangos better than any- body. My Aunt Pilar married El Moreno, who sang so well you could have eaten him. His mother, La Guaracha sang* por soleá *very well."*[45]

Rafael Romero, *El Gallina* -The Chicken- (b.1910-1991) recounted that at the age of twelve he was already a professional cantaor: *"In my family there were many singers, my mother, God rest her soul, and an aunt, but not professionally. My father played guitar, and my uncle too ... in the village, though they were not professionals."*[46]

El Camarón de La Isla said:

"In my house everybody sang, but not professionally. My father sang his Gypsy soleá and sigu- iriyas...Ay, his asthma bothered him! He didn't get it in the smithy, but from the years of hunger, working on the tramways on night and day shifts, and from getting rained on so often. My mother sang to drive you mad, with lots of personality. I can be proud of having learned every- thing from her. Well, from her and all the old artists who were all from La Isla and who used to drop into my house when they were passing through."[47]

Antonio Nuñez 'El Chocolate' (b. 1931) a Gypsy from Jerez says his parents sang and his brothers as well, but he is the only professional in his family.

Manuel Soto Monje 'Sordera de Jerez' (1927-2001) the patriarch of the Soto dynasty today, said his father sang well although he wasn't a professional, that his great Aunt was also a singer, and in his family there have always been singers *"who sang well; they weren't artists, but they sang. Lots of them."*[48] The term 'artists' here means professionals, those who earn money from their artistry.

---

[45]Fernando Quiñones: *Antonio Mairena, su Cante su Significado.*
[46]A.A.Caballero: *El Cante Flamenco.*
[47]*El Europeo* magazine N° 33, Interview by Francisco Rivas.
[48]A. A.Caballero, *El Cante Flamenco.*

As far back as 1784 and 85, a census recorded that 67% of Spain's Gypsies lived in Andalucia. Of these many Flamenco family names appear, such as the Vargas family married to the Montoyas in Lebrija and Arcos (Seville province), the Flores united with more Montoyas and with Monjes in Seville, Málaga and Jerez, and the Montoyas in Murcia, Alicante, Almería and Seville, Cádiz, Granada and Cordoba. These names reappear over and over throughout flamenco's history, giving rise to the theory that the very roots of flamenco reside in just a few Gypsy families who spread out between Seville and Cádiz.

There are also many recent flamencos who share these family names. In Spain it's customary to use both your father's and your mother's name, with the father's taking priority. In 2000 the law changed, and citizens may now choose whether to put their mother's name first on official documents. But the custom means that Fernando Fernández Monje 'El Terremoto de Jerez' (1934-1981) would be known officially as Fernando Fernández. José Monje Cruz 'El Camaron de La Isla' (1950-1992) is therefore also related to the Monjes, as is Manuel Soto Monje (b. 1927). José Soto Soto whose artistic name is José Mercé today, is the son of Francisco Soto Monje - El Sordera's brother- and is therefore El Sordera's nephew. The Montoya name shows up with Antonio Nuñez Montoya 'El Chocolate' (b. 1931) who shares it with the famous guitarist Ramón Montoya. Pepe Montoya 'Montoyita' is the maternal grandfather of Enrique Morente's cantaora daughter Estrella Morente. Among the Gypsy flamencos almost everybody is related to everybody else, which is perhaps why they often call each other 'cousin', just in case!

Of course, today not every person with one of these names is either Flamenco nor of Gypsy origin, nor even related to one of the flamenco dynasties.

CHAPTER 6: "TIME CARRIES IN IT'S SHAWL, MY TRUTHS"

WHAT ARE THEY SINGING ABOUT?

Listen to what I have to tell you, it hurts me even to talk. I am worn out from crying, I don't even dare to murmur. Time carries in it's shawl, my truths, embroidered. I have to forgive myself for sighing ... no one sighs for me.[49]

Sometimes asking 'what are they singing about?' is like looking for meaning in a sunset. To understand the song, it takes more than just a translation of the words, you have to tune into the feeling behind them. Some would say listening to flamenco is an art in itself, which is one reason why a difference is drawn between an appreciative amateur *aficionado*, and someone who recognises the different versions of a palo and other fine details, who is known as a *cabal*. But without knowing what the song's about, anyone can learn to appreciate the subtle nuances of the singer's voice as it breaks with extreme emotion, how he moves his hands, how he clutches at his shirt, opens and closes his fists and throws his arms backwards exposing his chest as though ready for the mortal blade. For many, such a primitive display of emotion is too strong, too much to bear. But for others around the world, regardless of their backgrounds and cultural origins, it reconnects them with something fundamental, with the essence of being human.[50]

Perhaps because the emotional context of the cante has been established for centuries, it doesn't matter whether the verses make sense. And as the number of non-Spanish speaking aficionados proves, it doesn't matter whether you understand what they're singing about or not. Camarón didn't understand a lot of the new verses written for him, let alone some of those quite surreal verses from García Lorca and other 'cultured' poets. But he was always able to imbue his cante with the emotion which ensured audiences identified with it.

Flamenco wouldn't have existed without the lyrics to the songs. In its early days the lyrics gave each *palo* its emotional content which survives even in the purely instrumental forms. Since the guitar has developed more complex harmonies emulating the cante, it too can be just as poetic as any jondo cantaor. One of the most interesting aspects of all music is the ability certain harmonies and chords have to prompt certain emotional states within the listener, regardless of what language is being sung.

When Mairena and Molina wrote *Mundo y Formas del Cante Flamenco* in 1963, they were already complaining about the degree of degradation the lyrics to el cante had suffered in the previous forty years. This was the result of the period in flamenco when it had been adapted to stage productions in theatres and on film, mixing folk and popular themes with romantic or dramatic stories. For example, the death of a miner's sons might be sung in a flamenco voice sometimes interspersed with recitation, with a style similar to what you might read in sensationalist press, manipulating the audience's emotions and sometimes interspersed with recitation, which Mairena classed as grotesque.

A flamenco voice hurts, there's something about it, a rawness which wounds. It's a bottomless well of emotions. No matter what words are sung, or whether you can understand them, the voice itself is full of suffering to begin with. A flamenco voice can awaken feelings in us we had buried and forgotten. A *cantaor* almost serves the role of a shaman, healing us by bringing us back in touch with the primitive source of our emotions. It has the power to re-humanize us in a world where feelings and passion have to be controlled or ignored.

---

[49]CD *De Santiago a Triana*, Flamenco Vive, Ethnic B6797
[50]Why are the songs so often about pain, sorrow and death? See Chapter 9, "What's the History?"

FLAMENCO DIALECT

Flamenco is only sung in the Andaluz dialect, not with the Castillian pronunciation of Spanish, nor with any other accent other than that of the Andaluz. Even though many famous Flamencos have come from the autonomous North Eastern region of Catalunya, and young stars like Miguel Poveda, Duquende or Maite Martin hail from Barcelona, none of them will ever sing with a Catalan accent or in anything other than Andaluz. The Spanish you hear in flamenco songs is often grammatically incorrect, like American slang or English. The Andaluz accent often substitutes an 'R' for an 'L' as in: *farda* instead of *falda* - skirt; or a 'G' for a 'V' -*güerta*, instead of *vuelta*- turn, and it swallows consonants like 'D' and 'R' as in *to'as* instead of *todas*- all; or *mejó* instead of mejor, *caló* instead of *calor*- heat. The original language of the Spanish Gypsies, coincidentally called *caló* today, is hardly spoken anymore and only a few words here and there turn up in el cante. Flamenco uses lots of slang terms from every day life and some of these are Gypsy terms which have been integrated into Andalucian speech. Like *chalao* which in slang today means nuts, daft, loony, it comes from the gypsy word *chalar*; to drive mad. Overwhelmingly, the lyrics to the songs are in Castillian Spanish, not caló, but when pronounced in the Andaluz dialect, it can sometimes sound like a different language.

The words in flamenco song are practically always deformed, unlike in Arabic singing for example, which is often assumed to be the origin of flamenco and in which the verse must always be clearly understood. The added syllables in Arabic and Arabigo-Andaluz music obey certain rules; any sung text has to be understood.[51]

A common habit is repetition. In Spanish, short phrases often get repeated for emphasis, for drama, to show understanding or amazement, and for the hell of it. Sometimes the rhythm of the phrase is pleasing in itself and it just feels good to repeat it. Ask someone a question in Andalucía, and they'll often repeat it back to you before answering:

"What's the name of this street?"

"What's the name of this street? This is the 'Street of the Sighs'."

Another of the mannerisms peculiar to flamenco is the opening *temple* or *ayeo* which help the cantaor prepare for his song. This is an aspect people unfamiliar with flamenco often joke about, perhaps in self defence, as the raw emotion conveyed is challenging and seems melodramatic. *Temple*[52] comes from the word *templar*- to tune up- and the singer uses this introduction to get in tune with the emotions necessary for the form he'll sing. Sometimes these are just a series of 'ayes', a versatile expression in Spanish which you can use interchangeably for joy or sadness. Sometimes it will develop into a heartfelt complaint, a *quejío*, from *quejar*- to complain. To complain in Spanish culture isn't as frowned upon as it is in Anglo cultures, so when the legendary cantaor Manuel Torres was said to 'complain better than he sang', it was one of the highest complements in flamenco.[53]

WHO WROTE THE SONGS?

Browsing through the shelves of the specialist store Flamenco Vive in Madrid one day, I overheard a conversation between the owner and two young women who were working on a project compiling the lyrics to songs by Spanish singer-songwriters. It was 1998, the year of the centenary of García Lorca's birth and Enrique Morente had just produced a CD called *Lorca*, in homage to the famous poet. Morente sets the lyrics from some of Lorca's most beautiful works to the flamenco compás of *tangos*, *rumba*, *granaína y taranta* and *bulerías*.

The young women explained their project, "We thought it would be interesting to include the authors

[51]See in Chapter 9, "Arabigo-Andaluz Tongue Twisters."

[52]The same term is used in bullfighting to describe the way a toreador engages the bull at the beginning of his *faena*.

[53]CD notes, J. Blas Vega, Sonifolk CD, *Manuel Torre*.

of flamenco lyrics," one of them said "Who writes the words to flamenco?" she asked. The owner seemed surprised at the question: "Well, nobody really writes them...," he faltered, he couldn't quite explain that most of the words you hear in a flamenco song have been handed down from generation to generation, and nobody knows who the original author was. The young woman tried putting her question a different way, "But, you know, whose words are they using? Like this one," she picked up Morente's CD which is clearly titled LORCA: "Who wrote the words to this?"

Flamenco originally served a social need; it was sung and danced to reinforce a sense of community and to relieve and share pain, sorrow and joy, and it has had to adapt to the changes in that community. Most of the lyrics to flamenco are still relevant to audiences today since they deal with universal emotions which can be interpreted by most cultures. For example, the expression of pain and frustration at losing a brother in the mines can be understood by everyone with a capacity for empathy, even though they may not have a brother, let alone ever have been near a working mine. If the interpreters can convey the fundamental emotional state within the traditional verse, then these will survive. But if the singer needs a more modern theme, something he can identify with, then new verses will be adapted to fit the traditional melodies and rhythms. Since the emotional content of the forms has long been established, changing the words carries the risk of changing the emotional context. Each performer must choose the words to the style he'll sing, according to its emotional context and according to his own mood, the best singer will make it seem as if he just thought up the words on the spot.

Some of the verses in flamenco are traditional. Some are originally a mixture of Romances, popular verse, and the lengthy *glosas* - poem songs- which date back to the 13th and 14th century. From the days of the Moorish occupation, through the Medieval and Romantic eras, right up to the present day, the same themes recur in popular verses and epic poems: The pastoral theme of the lost wanderer, the romantic view of life as a shepherd, or the joys of a farming life, for example. Some are based on religious poetry. The Romances were sometimes like news bulletins about historic events, like the retaking of Granada in 1492. Some of the lyrics in flamenco today still refer to historic events of the 1800's:

Mi marido no está aquí	My husband isn't here
que está en la guerra de Francia	He's in the war with France
buscando con un candíl	Searching with a candle
a una picara mulata	For a saucy dark girl
Salgan los canastitos	Bring out the little baskets
de San Juan de Dios	For San Juan de Dios
Pedí limosna pal entierro de Riego	I ask for alms for Riego's funeral
Que va de por Dios	For God's sake[54]
Baluarte invencible	Unconquerable fortress
Isla de León	The Isle of Leon
Cómo ganaron los franceses, mare	How did the French win, Mother?
Fue por una traición	It was because of treason[55]

[54]Refers to the death of Colonel Riego, See Chapter 9, "Politics and War."
[55]Refers to the Napoleonic invasion of Spain.

FLAMENCO POETS

A surprising amount of verses are actually formally 'composed', either by the singers themselves or by amateur or professional poets. José Cepero (1888-1960) was known as 'The Poet of El Cante' because many of the lyrics he sang were his own invention. Paco de Lucía's father was the author of many of Camarón de La Isla's verses. Pepe de Lucía, Paco's brother, is also a prolific songwriter for *el cante* and pop song. Various friends and admirers of Camarón also wrote verses for him, so not all the words in el cante are strictly traditional. Some are from formally composed poems. The poet Manuel Machado Álvarez, commonly known as M. Machado, wrote many verses which are so often sung in the *cantes* that their origin as poems has been forgotten. His father, Antonio Machado y Álvarez, put together the first collection of Gypsy *cantes* under the pseudonym *Demófilo*.[56] On recordings, these poems are simply called 'popular' verse. García Lorca has also been adopted by flamencos. Lorca was an 'aficionado' and a gifted musician who played guitar and piano, and many of his poems have an innate rhythm which easily fits a flamenco *compás*.

BY WORD OF MOUTH

The oral tradition of flamenco keeps a collective memory alive. Even today, many singers are illiterate, and it's hard for those of us brought up in a literate culture to imagine the advantages of this, but one of them is a better memory. Juana la del Revuelo[57] reads so poorly that her husband writes the words of her *cantes* for her using simple diagrams and pictures. Like many formally uneducated people, Camarón de La Isla often had difficulties pronouncing long words. During the recording of his last CD 'Potro de Rabia y Miel'[58], Camarón had such difficulty pronouncing 'laberinto' in the line *eres como un laberinto de pasiones*- you are like a labyrinth of passions–that they assigned it to the chorus of voices.[59]

Although most of the forms have themes, the lyrics are quite interchangeable between these. The verse from a soleá or an alegrías, for example, can also be sung in a bulerías, or the words in a seguiriyas may also be used in a soleá. The important thing is that the singer matches the emotional content appropriate to the song form with an appropriate delivery. Many songs have specific verses which are attributed to the cantaor or cantaora who made it popular. For example there are many Malagueñas named after the cantaor who first sang those words. Such as the Malagueñas del Mellizo originally sung by Enrique El Mellizo, or Malagueñas de Chacón after Don Antonio Chacón, or the Malagueñas Perotas. Therefore, the great number of variations on the Malagueña form can be identified by the words used and the melodic line established by the singer. The *malgueñas*, *rondeñas*, and *granaínas* are all thought to stem from regional fandangos, the *malagueñas* are therefore the *fandangos* from the province of Málaga and the *granaínas* from the province of Granada.

MALAGUEÑAS

If the *seguiriyas* is the original Gypsy cante to transmit grief beyond words in a primitive cry, the Malagueñas is the more intellectually poetic payo's (non-Gypsy's) vehicle to relieve himself in semi religious overtones, of anguish and despair. Among flamenco palos, the Malagueñas occupy a significant position as one of the richest and most demanding of cantes. Antonio Chacón is credited as the maestro responsible for developing them. Each malagueña is named after the cantaor who first sang the particular lyrics, and after the village it comes from. Therefore the vast number of variations can be identified by the lyrics.

---

[56] 1846-1893.

[57] Gypsy 'festera' born in Seville, 1952.

[58] Phillips CD 512-408-2 (1992).

[59] Camarón de La Isla, F. Peregil, *El País,* Aguilar 1993.

"I like to sing the cante por Malagueñas; if it is sung well, it can freeze your blood and make you burst out crying." So sings Diego Clavel in *"Malagueñas Perotas y del Niño de Vélez"*.[60] Álora is often cited as the village in the province of Málaga where the malagueñas originated; people from there are known as *Perotas*, therefore these Malagueñas are the originals from Álora. The malagueñas require a highly developed vocal technique and breath control, as the lines are very ornamented and full of drawn-out melismas. A structural peculiarity is that the first line of the verse is usually sung as the second line. By repeating the second line, the subject of the clause is always emphasised. For example: *"To ask God for forgiveness, I went into the temple, to ask God for forgiveness."* The guitar accompaniment is metric, and is basically always the same whether in the tone of a granaína, or taranto, and only when the cantaor begins the verse can you recognise whether he's singing a Malagueñas del Canario, or de Juan Breva or del Mellizo for example, or a personal creation of his own. These days, some verses of Malagueñas del Mellizo can regularly be heard in flamenco recitals:

A Dios yo le pido	Of God I am asking
por si me quiere escuchar	If he wishes to hear me
a Dios le estoy pidiendo	I am asking God
que tu me quieras a mi	That you should love me
como yo te estoy queriendo	As much as I am in love with you
si no, prefiero el morir	If not, I prefer death

As a guitar solo, the malagueñas has almost completely disappeared. Even Paco de Lucía recorded only one version in his entire discography to date. Its repetitive structure no longer satisfies the harmonically advanced musicality of today's soloists and it has been replaced by the Rondeñas. The guitar accompaniment provides few moments for the modern guitarist to show off; it requires an inventive and developed musicality to provide variety and imprint a personal stamp on the set pattern. The Rondeña is another fandangos based style which is practically never sung today; only the guitar version is played.[61] Once again, the name was thought to refer to the geographical origin of the style, so the Rondeña would be from Ronda. In Gerald Brenan's memoirs of his life in the Alpujarra mountains during the early 1920s[62] he recounts the custom among the villages for young men to 'do the rounds'- *hacer una ronda*- which could also be the origin of the term, since the songs they sung may have been called Rondeñas. He describes the boys serenading their girlfriends with a *copla*- a verse of four lines- which would make the girl get up and show herself at the window if she was flattered by it.

OCCUPATIONAL HAZARDS

Some forms have specific themes, like the group of styles from the Levante region which includes the *cartagenera* named after the mining town in the province of Murcia, the *minera* from La Union in Murcia where a prestigious competition is held every year, and the *tarantas* from Almería. All the *Cantes de Levante* - songs from the east- have the same source- the regional *fandango* and all of them abide by the harmonic structure of the fandangos. The ending 'ngo' is believed to have an African origin; hence zorongo, tango, and fandango originated in the dances of the Black slaves but no doubt went through a process of development and adaptation to reach us as we know them today. Although many different origins have been suggested, it seems most likely these styles were adapted gradually from the slaves in Latin America. The folkloric fandangos are

---

[60]CD *La Malagueña a Través de los Tiempos* Cambayá 012.F2.
[61]See Chapter 11; "Who were the Famous Guitarists?"
[62]*South From Granada*, Gerald Brenan Hamish Hamilton, London 1957.

not strictly considered flamenco, these are the ones with a 3/4 rhythmic base. The best known of these, which have been accepted into the flamenco umbrella are the fandangos de Huelva, de Alosno and the verdiales. Those which have a so-called 'free rhythm' are believed to be flamenco creations of such masters as Chacón: cartageneras, mineras, tarantas, granaínas and those called simply 'personal creations'.

The Taranta is a miner's lament:

Que tan despacito caminas,	You're walking so slowly,
Dime que llevas en el carro.	Tell me what you have in that cart.
"Llevo a mi pobre hermano,	"I am carrying my poor brother,
que un barreno en las minas,	A drill in the mines,
le ha cortao las dos manos."	Has cut off both his hands."

Many have tried to explain the term *tarantas* as being the fandangos originating in Almería arguing that people from Almería are called *tarantos*, which is only true in dictionaries. All of my family are from Almería and none of us has ever been called a *taranto*, and none of us refer to anybody else from Almería as such. Everybody in Spain calls them *Almerienses*.

Often, the names of things come from a mispronunciation or twisting of the original word into a local dialect. Thus in English, some people pronounce chimney as chimley, or say 'would of' instead of 'would have'. In Spanish the same thing happens, words like *croquetas* become *cocretas*, or *tela metálica* (wire mesh) gets squashed up together to become *telámica*. Some studies tried to find the origins of *tarantas* in the wild dance from Italy called the *Tarantella* , said to cure the effects of being bitten by a spider. But these arguments fail when confronted by the fact that musically the two forms have absolutely nothing in common.

In Spanish *tartanas* are the carriages gypsies and blacksmiths used; a *tartanero* is therefore a carriage driver. The words to the classic cartagenera illustrate this:

Un lunes por la mañana	One Monday morning
los picaros tartaneros	The cheeky carriage drivers
les robaron las manzanas	Stole the apples
a los pobres arrieros	From the poor mule drivers
que venían de Totana	Who had come from Totana

But this doesn't have any connection with the tarantas or tarantos either, which always have the same themes—mining:

De Cartagena a Almería	From Cartagena to Almería
de Linares a Cartagena	From Linares to Cartagena
donde nació la taranta	where the taranta was born
que conocemos hoy día	that we know today
y los mineros la cantan	and it is sung by the miners

In *Almería por Tarantas*[63], Antonio Sevillano Miralles traces the origin of the term *tarantos* and finds that as a reference to a flamenco form it dates only from the early 1900s. During the first mining boom of the late 1850s to 70s in Almería and neighbouring Murcia and Linares, the workers who migrated to these areas

---

[63]Instituto de Estudios Almerienses de la Diputación Provincial de Almería 1996.

were just called *Andaluzes*. Up until 1908, when Carmen de Burgos Seguí *Colombine,* the daughter of a mine owner, wrote about the working conditions of these men, the term had not been recorded in any dictionary and had not been used in reference to any musical form. In her report she writes of the abundance of workers from Almería and Granada calling them *Tarantos*. She includes a footnote explaining that this name probably arose from the comradeship between them, saying that the word derives from *estarán todos*- they will all be there- which when using the Andaluz dialect and dropping the letter 'd' sounds like *estarán tós* - hence *tarantos*. This may have originated in a song whose verse goes:

"Estarán tós los mineros?"	"Will all the miners be there?"
a preguntao el capataz	the manager asked
Estarán tós los mineros	All the miners will be there
De aqui voy a se un taranto	From now on I'm going to be a *taranto*
pá que ve mi capataz	So that my manager can see
con el salero que canto	How well I sing[64]

The *taranto* is in binary rhythm and can be danced, whereas all other fandangos flamencos have no set rhythm other than the 'internal' count of the singer. The themes of the tarantos, are less strongly associated with the mines:

Tanto como nos queremos	We love each other so much
y tratan de separarnos	and they try to separate us
Y es que no tienen conciencia	It's because they don't realise
ni saben lo que es amor	They don't know what love is
ni han pasao por su experiencia	And they haven't been through the experience

All of the flamenco fandangos share the same musical characteristic, the *granaína, malagueña* and *taranta* and *cartagenera* all start with the guitar introducing the Andalucian cadence,[65] but when the cante starts, they revert to traditional harmony.

FROM THE SUBLIME TO THE RIDICULOUS

The subjects of flamenco songs range from the deeply moving and poetic, to the nonsensical and ridiculous. Tomasa Guerrero Carrasco *La Macanita* nearly always sings these traditional *letras por bulerías:*

Mi amante es pajarero	*My lover is a bird seller*
Me trajo un loro	*He brought me a parrot*
con las alas doradas	*With golden wings*
y el pico de oro.	*And a golden beak*
Ay, mare, mare	*Ay mother, mother-*
Yo creí que llovía,	*I thought it was raining,*
pero agüita no cae.	*but the rain didn't come*

There is a clear difference between lyrics of Gypsy origin and those of a more structured poetic nature, from the more intellectual payo. The Gypsy's words are more direct and simple, expressing their feelings without hiding behind euphemisms. Those which come from the general Andalucian tradition of Romances and

---

[64]Idem.
[65]Flamenco Phrygian mode Amin-G- F- E.

popular verse and even refrains are more literary and ambiguous, drawing analogies or describing beauty in a poetic way. Compare these two verses; the first one is straightforward, the second, more poetic:

Soy desgraciaíto.	How damned I am–
hasta en el andá.	even in the way I walk.
Que los pasitos que pa'lante doy	The steps I take forward
Se me van p'atrás.	take me backward.

Como tortolíta	Like a little dove
te fui yo buscando,	I went looking for you
compañerita, de olivo en olivo	my dear friend, from olive tree to olive tree
de ramito en ramo.	from branch to branch

Or these simple statements:

No sé que tiene	I don't know what the mint
la yerbagüena de tu huerto	in your garden has
que tan bien me huele	that makes it smell so good to me

Dime tú, Dolores,	Tell me, Dolores,
¿Con que te lavas la cara	What do you wash your face with
que tanto te güele a flores?	that it smells so of flowers?

The flamenco we hear today in live performances and on recordings is subtly changing all the time. The styles considered the roots of everything, the *soleares* and *seguiriyas* above all, are undergoing changes which may or may not be adopted generally to become the *new* standard. The old recordings of past masters show us their different interpretation of the basic *compás* and harmonies, and by listening to these we can follow the evolution of styles. The *bulerías,* for example used to be considered a frivolous style; called a *chufla* it was neither as popular nor as fast as today when we have at least three recognisable styles of performance: those of Utrera, Jerez and Seville. The *seguiriyas* is another style whose evolution we can trace through recordings, it used to be far more monotonous both vocally and harmonically.

Almost every flamenco form shares a particular characteristic with another. For example the *soleá, alegrías* and *bulerías* all share the same rhythmic cycle or *compás*. The *tangos, tanguillo* and *tientos* are also the same, one being a slow version of the other, and the flamenco rumba is closely related rhythmically to the tanguillo.

TANGOS

Like the fandangos and zorongo, the name tango at least may have an African origin. Today the origins are accepted as being the Black African dances brought back from Cuba and other Spanish colonies. The earliest mentions of the tango place it in the ports of Cádiz and Seville where traffic to and from the Americas set sail. Hence there are the tangos de Cádiz, and de Triana. But this tangos dance style often described in accounts of early 19th century travellers was not the flamenco tangos. La Niña de Los Peines, who owes her nickname (The Girl of the Combs) to a tangos she became famous for, is credited with the development of the flamenco tangos:

Péinate tú con mis peines	Comb your hair with my combs
Que mis peines son de azucar.	My combs are made of sugar
Quién con mis peines se peina,	He who uses my combs,
hasta los dedos se chupa.	even sucks his fingers
No te metas en quereres	Don't get mixed up in love
porque se pasa mucha fatiga	because you'll have a bad time-
Mira si yo vivo con pena	Look at me, how I live in pain,
que estoy muerta estando viva	that I'm dead although I'm alive.

The tanguillos ('little tangos') are faster and more closely related to the rumba rhythm. The lyrics to these are also more light hearted and related to the carnival tradition in Cádiz, where groups of non-professionals called *comparsas* get together to compose and sing songs which are full of fun and sarcasm.

Tientos The tientos are a slow tangos. Don Antonio Chacón is credited with establishing the final version of this form which combines the *jondura* of a seguiriyas with the rhythm of a slow tangos:

La luz del entendimiento	The grace of understanding
tu me has estao dando a comprender	you've been making me understand
Que no hay fatigas mas grandes	There is no greater suffering
que aquel que quiere y no pue	than he who wants to but cannot

Lots of styles mentioned in programs and reports of the early days of flamenco have fallen by the way-side; some singers today claim to be the only ones keeping certain styles alive. A lot of flamenco seems to be attributable to a handful of singers from the early 1800s who were the first known professionals. Sometimes the singer responsible for a particular style wasn't sufficiently known for others to hear him and learn his interpretation, which would have assured the continuation. Sometimes the social context of the lyrics has been forgotten and its relevance is lost, so the style is not sung anymore. Like the old ploughing songs, the *trilleras* were not just sung in a flamenco style, but all over the country where farmers used traditional farming methods. The *trilleras* would be sung while standing on a *trilla*, a slab of wood with pieces of flint stuck in it drawn by mules or horses. Hauled around a tight circular platform, the *trilla* or *tabla* was used to separate the wheat grain from the chaff. These days you'll find old *trillas* turned upside down, with the sharp bits covered by a thick pane of glass to create fancy coffee tables! The *trilleras* songs don't have the same significance when you're sitting in the seat of a tractor. Another example might be the songs of the professional mourners, the *plañideras* following a funeral cortege....yet, the wailing style of deep loss which became the *seguiriyas* is still appreciated.

WHAT'S IN A SEGUIRIYAS?

The name *seguiriya* is thought to be an Andaluz pronunciation of Seguidilla. *Seguida* means 'following', from the verb *seguir-* 'to follow.' There is a different type of Seguidilla, a popular song and dance often called *seguidilla bolera,* dating from the early 16th century and there's plenty of evidence proving its popularity continued throughout the 18th century when flamenco was becoming a professionalised art form. This seguidillas boleras is mentioned in the writings of Cervantes and those of English travellers to Spain: George

Borrow, Joseph Townsend, Henry Swinburne and Richard Ford, not to mention Charles Davillier and Hans Christian Andersen. Some writers and theorists have assumed that the flamenco seguiriyas stems from the folkloric seguidillas, but the differences between the popular *seguidilla* and the flamenco or Gypsy *seguiriya* are so great, it's almost impossible to find a common link between them.

The Seguidillas is an energetic and lighthearted style, sung and danced in order to lighten the soul and entertain. It's based on a common 3/4 timing. The *compás* of the flamenco *seguiriya* consists of three fast beats with two slow ones distributed across a twelve beat cycle (compás). There's no consensus as to how to write this yet, and as the seguiriyas is now being played with a faster pace, it is drawing closer to the 12 beat compás of a bulerías, but with a different emphasis. Like almost all flamenco forms it's an amalgam of rhythms superimposed on one another. The guitar sets the scene for the *seguiriyas* with a dramatically emphatic and slow introduction. There are many, many moments during the cycle when the singer is quiet, and the guitar repeats a simple slow pattern, which by it's nature draws the listener into a meditative seriousness.

The flamenco song form has been linked with the *toná* , (the Andalucian pronunciation of 'tonada') a family of unnacompanied songs with the same rhythmic peculiarities as the seguiriya, a rhythm based on the syllables of the lyrics. *Tonadas, tonás, or tonadillas* (they're all the same thing) was the name given to popular songs all over Spain.[66] Each village or region had its own *tonada* with its own name. The flamenco toná is in turn linked with the *endecha*, which was a lament on the death of a loved one sometimes sung by professional mourners known as *plañideras* or *playeras,* women hired to cry at funerals.[67] These professional mourners were known as *seguidillas playeras*, in other words; 'those who weep following the funeral'. In fact, within flamenco, the terms *seguiriya* and *playera* used to be interchangeable.

Antonio Mairena, is credited with recreating the *tonás-seguiriyas* which begin with the same introduction from the guitar as the *seguiriyas*, but continue without guitar accompaniment. He also gave different regional names to the seguiriyas sung in different towns, even though the differences between them are sometimes negligible and only someone living in that particular town might pinpoint them. Sometimes it's just the words that are different, for example the *Seguiriyas de Cádiz y los Puertos* usually have some reference to the sea. Others, such as the *Seguiriyas de Triana* (the neighbourhood in Seville with a rich flamenco tradition) have religious references, and the guitar accompaniment in these snakes between major and minor whereas all other *seguiriyas* are in the minor mode. Some writers have suggested that the *seguiriya* used to be completely rhythm less, until the dancer Vicente Escudero (1885-1980) developed it for the dance. Since he had to learn the uneven 12 beat rhythm from the guitarist Gabriel Ruíz[68] in order to dance to it, obviously the rhythm existed before he adapted it for dance steps.

Antonio Mairena and Ricardo Molina described the seguiriyas as the song of the hopeless cry. Today, cantaores will offer a *seguiriyas* as though it were a simple matter, in which case they're probably not doing the style or themselves justice. It involves the sort of feelings one can't just conjure up, like an actor reciting a passage from Shakespeare out of context. If you hear a *cantaor* say, "And now I am going to sing a little bit *por seguiriyas*," after only one or two *cantes*, you may well be disappointed to find he doesn't give you goose bumps, or raise the hair on the back of your neck with his interpretation, despite everything you've heard about how dark and soul-baring the *seguiriyas* is supposed to be. Most professional singers just go through a selection of *cantes*, like any other musician in a prepared concert running through his programme. Very few of them delve deep enough to reach those dark sounds which stay in your ears for a long time.

---

[66] See Chapter 7, "Disembodied Reasoning"
[67] Hipolito Rossy, in his *Teoría del cante jondo*, remembers the plañideras of the village of Osuna, Seville in 1905.
[68] Paco Sevilla, "Queen of the Gypsies," *The Life and Legend of Carmen Amaya*, 1999.

The *seguiriyas* is the most tragic, dark and despairing of all the cantes. The lyrics are always profound, dealing with imprisonment and loss, the death of a loved one, of love itself, of hope, or of a holy figure. The *tercios*, words or lyrics to the *seguiriyas* are often deeply poetic, sometimes striking in their simplicity, and always dramatic and emotionally charged.

SPLITTING SYLLABLES

The verses of a seguiriyas are built on two short lines followed by one long one, then ending with another short line. The syllables of the words are what give it the rhythm, the cyclical *compás*. The first two lines are made up of words with 6 syllables, the third line has 11, and the last one has 6 again. Like everything else in flamenco, these rules are never strictly adhered to, and in practise you get seguiriyas in all sorts of syllable counts. When you hear a cantaor singing a *seguiriyas*, it's not easy to count the syllables. Sometimes they make up the numbers by splitting, or adding to the existing ones. Like the word *derramado* (der-ra-ma-do) 'overflowed', which is transformed in Andaluz and flamenco dialect to de-rra-ma-i-to, thus adding a beat to its usual 4 syllables. Other additions include the common lament 'Ay!' which can get stretched out across as many syllables as you like in what's called a *melisma*, one vowel travelling through several notes. But despite this semi-scientific analyses of the seguiriyas, in fact, it is the octosyllable which predominates in flamenco song just as in the old Romances and most popular poetry. It seems to be the natural rhythm for spoken Spanish and makes up the majority of flamenco verses.

Here's a few examples of *letras por seguiriyas*:

Mi ropita vendo	I am selling my clothes
¿Quien me la quiere comprar?	Who wants to buy them from me?
Como la vendo por poquito dinero	I am selling them for little money
Pa' tu libertad	For your freedom

And this verse which is supposed to have come originally from Tomás El Nitri[69]:

Por aquella ventana	Through that window
Que al campo salía	Looking out onto the fields
Le daba voces a la mare de mi alma	I called out for the mother of my soul
Y no me respondía	And she did not answer me.

---

[69]See Chapter 4, "Flamenco's Founding Fathers."

On his 1992 CD: 'Negra Si Tu Supieras',[70] Enrique Morente sings these traditional lyrics;

EL VAPORCITO (The little engine)

Dios mio,¿qué es esto?	My God, what is this?
¿como sin frio ni calenturita,	As though without cold nor warmth,
me estoy muriendo?	I am dying?
Que latidos más grandes	What great beats
da mi corazon	My heart is pounding;
Si tu vieras mi cuerpo por dentro,	If you could see inside my body,
te diera dolor.	You would feel pain.
Fatigas me dieron,	It made me hurt,
Ganas de llorar,	Made me want to weep,
Cuando la vi en el vaporcito,	When I saw her in the little steam engine,
La máquina andar.	The engine pulling away.

HISTORIC SEGUIRIYEROS

A cantaor who sings the seguiriyas well is almost automatically considered a master, since this style is flamenco's emblematic palo. To sing it at all is a challenge for all cantaores and most young stars today are ultimately judged upon their rendition of seguiriyas, soleares and bulerías, contrasting styles which share the same basic compás.

The legendary cantaor El Fillo (b. circa 1820) was revered for his *seguiriyas*. El Fillo's voice has lent itself to flamenco terminology. The rough, almost worn out voice so many *cantaores* (and even *cantaoras*) have, is called a voice like Fillo's; *una voz afillá*. The story goes, that he was fond of children and always surrounded by them, so much so that La Andonda, said to be his lover, invented a verse which goes:

La Andonda le dijo al Fillo: ¡ Anda y vete, gallo ronco, a cantar a los chiquillos!
-"La Andonda said to El Fillo, Go on, get out of here you hoarse chicken, go sing to the kids!"[71]

One of the children who used to get close to Fillo when he sang, was Silverio Franconetti (whose birth and death dates were only recently confirmed as 1823–1889), the son of an Italian father serving in the Spanish army, and a Spanish mother. Silverio is said to have learned to sing flamenco at the feet, and indeed in the lap, of the master El Fillo. As a *payo* (non-Gypsy), and part Italian, Silverio is an unusual legend within flamenco. He's often referred to as the greatest cantaor of all time,[72] and much of his style and the verses he sang have come down through the generations to the present day. Silverio was one of the first to open a café cantante where flamenco was staged and performers were paid, and therefore one of the first to professionalise the art. Federico García Lorca, the famous poet, wrote of Silverio:

---

[70]*Nuevos Medios*, 15 602 (1992).
[71]La Andonda was El Fillo's companion; a respected singer of soleares herself, she died in Seville in 1878.
[72]As are Manuel Torres, don Antonio Chacón, Antonio Mairena and ultimately, Camarón!

Su grito fue terrible	His cry was terrifying
Los viejos	The old ones
dicen que se erizaban los cabellos,	Say it made their hair stand on end,
y se abría el azogue	And the mercury flowed
de los espejos.	From the mirrors.

As a *seguiriyero*, it's said he exceeded all expectations. The *seguiriyas* is the cante to sing when you are beyond consolation, when no words will express the torment and anguish inside. When one of Silverio's sons died, a friend visited to see how he was doing. Silverio replied:

"Imagine how I feel. I have spent the night lost and alone, singing seguiriyas...."[73]

Another story recounts how on his way to San Fernando in the province of Cádiz, passing the cemetery where his friend Enrique Ortega, another respected cantaor, was buried, Silverio stopped the carriage and simply sang this verse of *seguiriya*:

Por Puerta de Tierra	I don't want to pass by Puerta de Tierra,
yo no quiero pasar.	
Me acuerdo de mi amigo Enrique,	I remember my friend Enrique,
y me hecho a llorar.	And I start crying.

This verse may have been his variation on the verse spoken by his master, El Fillo:

Por la iglesia mayor no quiero pasar	I don't want to pass the church
Porque me acuerdo de la mare mía	Because I remember my mother
Y me hecho a llorar	And I start crying

WHAT'S IN AN ALEGRÍAS?

The *alegrías* always have happy and carefree themes, often about the sea, sailing, fishing and events related to the Napoleonic wars of 1808-1813. The theory is that during this time, soldiers from the Northern territories of Spain came down to Cádiz to fight the French invaders, bringing their regional songs and dances. Notably the jota, of which there are many regional variations. The four verses of the *alegrías* show that, like the Sevillanas, it is derived from a folkloric form of verse, and that the subjects and syllabic rhythms of the verses coincide with those of the *jota*.

Que desgraciaíto fuiste,	What bad luck you had,
un barrio con tanta gracia	A neighbourhood with such grace
qué de bombas recibiste.	And what a bombardment you took.

Aunque pongan en tu puerta	Even if they put artillery canons
cañones de artilleria,	in front of your door,
tengo que pasar por ella	I would have to come to it
aunque me cuesta la vida	even though it might cost me my life.

[73]J. Blas Vega: *Silverio Rey de los Cantaores,* Ed. La Posada 1995.

But if it were just an adaptation of a *jota*, why doesn't it sound anything like a *jota*? The origins must be a little more complex than simply adapting a northerner's neighbourhood song and dance to a flamenco way of singing. Its music is rhythmically the same as a *soleares* or *bulerías* i.e a 12 beat cycle with accents on the 3rd, 6th, 8th, 10th and 12th beats, which has nothing to do with the common 3/4 time of most jotas. The key is exactly the opposite of the soleá: a major mode rather than a minor. The *alegrías* is therefore like an opposite of the *soleares*. It has a jaunty brightness which contrasts with the dark soleá. It's possible a guitarist simply decided to play the *soleares* in a major key to accompany the lighter words of the *alegrías* song form.

WHAT'S IN A SOLEÁ?

Like the seguiriyas, the soleá is thought to contain the very essence of *flamencura*. And like the seguiriyas, the soleares group is made up of several contrasting styles from the different regions: the soleares of Triana, for example or the soleá de Jerez, de Lebrija, de Alcalá de Guadaira, de Cádiz y los puertos, de Marchena, Córdoba the soleá por bulerías or the soleá apolá. As with other flamenco palos, many of the differences are purely due to references in the words sung, but sometimes also because of a particular harmonic difference in the guitar accompaniment. Today, the soleá is invariably used by guitar teachers to introduce their students to the complexities of flamenco compás, since its rhythmic structure is used in the bulerías and alegrías, and all of the forms which generate from these: cantiñas, mirabrás, romeras, and bamberas.

The words to the soleares are full of references to love and frustrated lovers, to the maternal figure and her demise as well as personal suffering from illness usually caused by a lost love or bereavement. The soleares are also among the most immediate of the flamenco forms, in that the words often refer directly to personal experience of the singer, rather than generalised suffering. They vary between two and four verses:

Estrella Morente sings these *letras* (lyrics) attributed to Soleares de Chacón[74]:

Solamente con mirarte	Just by looking at you
comprenderás que te quiero	You will know that I love you
también comprenderás	You'll also understand
que quiero hablarte,	That I want to talk to you
y no puedo	But I can't

And Enrique Morente, her father, sings these traditional lyrics[75]:

El querer que tu me mostrabas	The love you showed for me
Como era de polvo y arena	Since it was of dust and sand
El aire se lo llevaba	The wind has taken it away

Fernanda de Utrera is most famous for her version of soleares:

Grande gustito tu habias tenio	You've been enjoying yourself
que has estao mandando en mi	Ordering me about
como bien te camelo	Every which way you wanted
to el tiempo que tu has querio	For as long as you wanted

---

[74]*Mi Cante y un Poema Virgin*, Chewaka 8102052.
[75]*Esencias Flamencas,* Ethnic Auvidis B 6151.

Cualquier día menos pensao	Any day when you least expect it
que este flamenco se entere	This Flamenco will find out
yo le voy a dar de lao	I'll walk right by him
¿Que quieres de mi	What do you want from me
si hasta el agüita que yo bebo	even for the water I drink
te la tengo que pedir?	I have to ask your permission?

Common words you'll hear in soleares are:

Me dicen que eres la ciencia	They tell me you are the wise one
Y yo no lo entiendo así	But I don't think that's right
Cómo siendo tu la ciencia	How come if you're so wise
No me has entendido a mi	You haven't understood me?
El querer quita sentido,	Love makes you lose your senses,
lo digo por experiencia,	I say this from experience,
porque a mi me ha sucedido.	Because it has happened to me.
Me muero yo,	I am dying,
De pena voy a morirme yo,	Of sorrow I'm going to die,
como me muero mordiendo la corteza	Just as I die biting the skin
del verde limon.	Of a green lemon.
Yo te quiero tanto,	I love you so much,
¿Que le voy a hacer?	What can I do?
Que yo apartarme de la verita tuya	For to leave your side,
Que no tengo poder.	I don't have the strength.

CHAPTER 7: WHAT'S THE GYPSY'S STORY?

DISEMBODIED REASON

Everything we know about the history of flamenco is written by *payos*, therefore from the non-Gypsy perspective. Antonio Mairena, (1909-1983) a Gypsy cantaor from the village of Mairena del Alcor near Seville, was the first to put forward an explanation of flamenco from the Gypsy point of view. In 1963 in collaboration with the poet Ricardo Molina he wrote 'Mundo y Formas del Cante Flamenco', perhaps the single most important book on flamenco to this day. He also published articles for newspapers and specialised magazines. Some people doubt the authenticity of his ideas; since he had no formal education, they doubted a mere Gypsy could be an intellectual. He distinguished between Gypsy flamenco and non-Gypsy flamenco, calling the one *Gitano-Andaluz* song forms, and the other Flamenco. He wasn't the first to do this. Antonio Machado y Alvarez *Demófilo,* the first serious writer on flamenco, made the same distinction in 1881.[76] In the 1920's the classical musician and composer Manuel de Falla continued to see a difference, calling flamenco a degeneration of the true art which was *Cante Jondo*.[77] His views were shared by the poet García Lorca and other intellectuals of the day who were passionate aficionados.

Antonio Mairena used the term *La Razón Incorpórea*, roughly "Disembodied Reasoning," which he claimed was something only Gypsies possessed. He was the first to talk about this 'Gypsy lore', and it seems he was trying to express a concept which is very hard for Gypsies to talk about. According to Mairena, it's the creed by which the Spanish Gypsy lives:

"It is our honour, the basis for Gypsy culture, all of our traditions and ancient rituals.
It's something only a Gypsy can understand, as God decrees, and which only Gypsies live ... it's
something untransferable, and unintelligible to outsiders ... it is the source of our inspiration
for el cante *and the Gypsy* cantaor, *and he expresses it in an intuitive way, via the* duende."

Carried away by his new found position as Gypsy spokesman, Mairena went so far as to declare that non-Gypsies could not sing nor perform flamenco well. Even the legends such as Chacón and Silverio were actually poor singers, according to him. How could they be any good, since they were not Gypsies? But, one of the enduring characteristics of Gypsies is their spontaneity, and any declaration can easily be contradicted in the next breath, as Mairena proved when he praised other non-Gypsy singers such as Fosforito.[78] Ever since *Mundo y Formas del Cante Flamenco* was published, flamencologists have either accepted or grappled with Mairena's assertions, which actually have no solid scientific basis to support them. Although the author's attempts to dignify and categorise flamenco can be applauded, it is also now being recognised that Mairena was not in fact equipped with any evidence to justify his declarations. Mairena and Molina considered that cantes–all of flamenco–could be categorised in four different groups, the first of which, *Cantes Basicos*–Basic Styles, they deemed to comprise the *"siguiriya, soleá, toná and tango which we esteem to be basic cantes because they are."* How's that for a scientific statement? This is children's playground science, needing no methical research to back it up.

According to Blas Vega, the *toná* is the flamenco term for *tonada*, a traditional folkloric song form of the village, from which arose the *tonadillas* composed and performed in the theatres of the 1600s - 1800s and whose ultimate derivation is the *cuplé*.[79] The musicologist García Matos stated that in many villages of

---

[76]*Colección de Cantes Flamencos,* 1881.
[77]See Chapter 3, *How Deep is Deep?*
[78]*Antonio Mairena Su Obra, Su Significado.* F. Quiñones.
[79]Blas Vegas notes in *Magna Antologia.*

Extremadura, Andalucia, and Castilla y Leon the word *toná* or *tonada* was always used to refer to a traditional song. When referring to the songs of their own regions they would call them *La toná de Ronda*, or *La Toná de las bodas* (Wedding Song), or *del columpio* (Swing Song) etc. The precursor to the *toná* is the romance, which has no guitar accompaniment. Tío Luís de la Juliana was supposedly the first specialist in *tonás*. A *toná* flamenca supposes an adaptation of an existing style or song to a 'new' flamenco style.

In 1954 the guitarist Perico el del Lunar organised and recorded the first anthology of flamenco cantes. One of the categories is *Cantes Matrices* or basic styles which includes the *caña, polo, soleares, seguiriyas* and *cabales*. This recording is deemed to mark the beginning of the phase of 'reevaluation' of flamenco after the Opera Flamenca period[80], along with books such as Gonzalez Climent's *Flamencología,* and Mairena and Molina's *Mundo y Formas*. Perico was one of a handful of flamenco artists who truly knew flamenco forms inside out, a cabal, and his aim was partly to ensure the survival of styles which had become unfashionable. He found the singers who still knew such old styles as the *marianas* and *cantes de trilla* which are almost never sung today, and instructed others whose memory or knowledge of a particular style was hazy or mistaken. Pepe el de la Matrona, like Perico, still knew and practised the old forms such as the *liviana* and *serranas* and contrary to what Antonio Mairena would have us believe of his prowess as guardian of *El Flamenco Puro* it was in fact Matrona who taught Mairena the *liviana,* although it must be said Mairena developed it musically beyond Matrona's original. Mairena's assertion that the *tonás* are the "Mother of All Cantes" is questionable, since before the release of Perico's *Antologia del Cante Flamenco*: *"We had never heard the tonás, and we didn't know of a single aficionado who knew them."*[81]

ARE ALL FLAMENCOS GYPSIES?

Today, one of Mairena's accompanists, Manuel Morao (b.1929) a Gypsy guitarist from the flamenco neighbourhood known as Santiago in Jerez, seems to still be suffering from a heavy dose of *Mairenismo*. He told us that everything in contemporary flamenco is rubbish, since everybody is ignoring the fundamental roots which one can only gain from racial identity, and which originate in the geographical location somewhere between Sevilla (specifically the neighbourhood of Triana), and Cádiz. He said:

> *"You have all been brain washed by that bunch of critics who decided Silverio was a great cantaor. Silverio was a non-Gypsy, a* gachó *who learned from El Fillo and from Tomás el Nitri. I have heard more good* cante *than those critics. How could they tell what Silverio's cante was like? Silverio sang like a* gachó *who learned to sing from the Gypsies."*

Silverio Franconetti was not a Gypsy[82], but he is responsible for the cultivation and popularisation of many standard flamenco forms. He founded one of the first *cafés cantantes* in Seville which were the venues where flamenco first became a professional art.

> *"I've never said all of this before,"* Morao went on: *"but I've had it up to here. Flamenco can only be sung and performed from the experience of a life time and Gypsies themselves have lost respect for this, and all those flamencos and all those 'evolutionists'. Not even Tia Añica nor Borrico were great artists, they were a part of it, almost ordinary, the simplest part. How could they be any good? They didn't have the artistic capacity that existed before them."*[83]

---

[80]See Chapter 9, "What's The History?"
[81]Jorge Martínez Salazar in *Perico El del Lunar "Un Flamenco de Antología* J.M Gamboa 2001.
[82]See Chapter 4, "Flamenco's Founding Fathers".
[83]*Alma Cien* magazine N° 15, June 2000.

Tía Añica la Piriñaca (1899-1987) was considered the guardian of the Jerez styles of soleares and seguiriyas. Manuel Morao actually accompanied her during many appearances throughout her career, which she only took up on the death of her husband. Antonio Mairena contracted her to sing on his 1965 anthology of flamenco and Gypsy song 'Antologia del cante flamenco y cante gitano' so presumably *he* thought she had good enough capacity and artistry. El Borrico (1910-1983) also took up a professional career late in life and was one of the most highly praised cantaores in his day. In 1984, his home town dedicated a street in his name.

And when asked who were the good artists, Morao clammed up and said cryptically: *"That's something you're never going to know, because I'm not going to tell you. You want to know lots of things, but we have to keep something to ourselves. That's why flamenco is so mistaken now, you have wanted to know everything, you have asked all the questions. Do you know what we have done? Half the time we've lied to you and the other half we've told the truth. That's why you're so mixed up."*

Obviously Morao, born in 1929, could never have heard either El Fillo (b.?-d.1878), El Nitri (b.1850?), nor Silverio who died in 1889, before the advent of sound recording. So his statements appear full of *anti-payo* sentiments, trying to maintain that flamenco is a purely Gypsy phenomenon. But what he said also reinforces the theory of a secretive period of flamenco, a time when only Gypsies performed it, before it "came out of the closet" and joined other entertainments.

Antonio Mairena's conviction that flamenco was an exclusively Gypsy invention is not shared by everybody, Gypsy or *payo*. Manuel Soto Monje 'El Sordera de Jerez' (1927-2001) was the patriarch of a Gypsy Flamenco dynasty from one of the traditionally flamenco neighbourhoods of Jerez. Asked whether he thought flamenco was Gypsy or *payo,* he said:

> *In my opinion it's neither Gypsy nor payo. The only thing I think el cante should have is that the interpreter singing the cante should have 'heart', or 'voice' or a way of singing to transmit it to the listeners, and give value to what he's singing. But not payo or Gypsy or anything, for me that doesn't exist. Maybe I can't explain it because I think that in Jerez there's such little difference between Gypsies and payos, it seems that since we grew up together, Gypsies and payos, there's no racial difference. There are gachós that I see singing por bulerías and they sing well, really well, and they come out dancing, really dancing, and another will come out por soleá and maybe one is a doctor, the other is a pastor, another is a mechanic. And I listen to them sing, and I revel in it because it's not Gypsy nor payo nor anything, they sing well and that's it.*[84]

THE PHARAOHS OF SPAIN?

Most books about flamenco and Gypsies quote 1425 as the year they came to Spain from France via the Pyrenees. A document from King Alfonso V of Aragón, which granted safe conduct to a "Duke of Little Egypt," proves this. The confusion of mistaken identities began right there, since Little Egypt -*Egipto Menor* - was what most of the Eastern Mediterranean, including Syria, Greece, and Cyprus was called during the Medieval ages. The Gypsies did not come from Northern Africa at all, but from the lands of the Ottoman Empire. Because the Gypsies declared themselves as having come from Little Egypt, they were called *Egipcios* or *Egiptanos* and it's thought the Spanish term *Gitano* evolved from *Egiptanos*. the legend is so deeply entrenched that even now, Gypsies themselves still sometimes say the pharaohs were their ancestors. *"La Faraona* - The Pharao-ess-, or *El Faraón* -..." the Pharaoh- are popular nickname among Flamencos, with all that they suggest about status, nobility and rank. Carmen Linares sings these lyrics to a bulerías[85]:

[84]*El Cante Flamenco,* A.A.Caballero
[85]*La Mujer en el cante,* Carmen Linares, CD, Mercury 532 397-2.

En los tiempos del Rey Faraón	In the days of the King Pharaoh
ese padrecito de la raza mía	That father of my race
celebraron su coronación	They celebrated his coronation
quatro gitanos que tanto querían...	Four Gypsies he loved so much...

The late Lola Flores who performed with Manolo Caracol from 1945 to 1952, was nicknamed *La Faraona* after a film she made in Mexico. It was her favourite nickname because she felt it identified her more closely as Gypsy even though she was only part Gypsy herself[86]. The poet Rafael Alberti recounted that the legendary Gypsy cantaor Manuel Torre (1878-1933) once said that in *el cante jondo,* what you must always search for until you find it is the: "black trunk of the Pharoah"-whatever that means.

The original bands of Gypsies who began arriving in Spain and the rest of Europe during the early 1400s, were usually made up of around 100 people or so led by a clan leader who would sometimes call himself a "duke" or a "prince." They were described as dressed in elaborate and colorful clothes and claimed to be of noble decent. Today, it is thought they originated in the area of Northern India and Pakistan known as the Punjab, because there are so many Punjabi words in the Gypsy language. But it has also been found that "many facts suggest their similarity and an origin in central India"[87] because of linguistic similarities with the languages of this area. It has also been theorised that they belonged to the Rajput caste, which even today symbolise the warrior class in India. Some say the Spanish Gypsies are descended from the *kshatriyas*, members of the second caste of Hinduism, -originally from the area now known as Rajasthan in North West India. It is not known why they left their homeland in the first place, except that the area was going through continual political power struggles. Within most Gypsy communities (they vary so much from one country to another that it's impossible to talk about one Gypsy group) there are strict rules about cleanliness and pollution. Tasks for men and women are strictly defined, mixing with non-Gypsies is thought to taint them, and certain tabus are similar to the complex caste system in India.

These Gypsies may have joined other traditionally nomadic people as they travelled about. They arrived in England in 1514, but well before that, in the 12th Century there was already a distinct nomadic group in Scotland who had their own identity and language, called Tinkler or Tynkers.[88] The word 'tinker' —one who travels about mending pots and pans and collecting scraps of metal- has come to be synonymous with "Gypsy" in most of the British Isles. In any event, by the time they arrived in Spain, they had no national identity, no possessions, no income, and no 'fixed abode'.

ETHNIC CLEANSING; BY ROYAL DECREE

For a while, the Gypsies in Medieval Spain were tolerated, until the Catholic Kings decided to persecute them in the same way they had persecuted the Moors and the Jews. Society lumped together the ordinary vagabond or vagrant, along with deserters from royal armies, highwaymen and nomads and called them all Gypsies. The authorities were upset by the Gypsies apparent displays of wealth, their colourful clothing and jangling gold bracelets and earrings. They wanted an orderly society where it was easy to see who was rich and who was poor, who was in authority and who was under the yoke. And so they banned Gypsies from wearing their traditional clothing, and they were officially forbidden from most kinds of work except farming, and allowed to live only in a few places in Andalucia: in the cities of Seville, Ecija and Carmona in the province of Seville and in the Puerto de Santa María in the province of Cádiz.

[86]*Los Nombres Artisticos en El Mundo Flamenco,* Ediciones Giralda 1997.
[87]J.P. Liégeois Gypsies: An Illustrated History, Al Saqi books London 1986.
[88]Idem.

Since nobody knew exactly where they came from, unlike the Moors they could hardly be 'sent home'. Instead, all sorts of laws were decreed to try to force them to settle in one area and conform to society. By 1637 slaves from Africa were in short supply, so they began sending convicted prisoners and Gypsies to the galleys. Royal decrees were issued against all those who called themselves Gypsies: punishments ranged from public flogging and the separation of men and women, to disfigurement (cutting off their ears), imprisonment and forced labour. They were forbidden from speaking their own language, and forced to register with local authorities or leave the country, and forbidden from marrying.

Antonio Mairena claimed the *Alboreá*, a song and dance traditionally performed at Gypsy weddings, should never be performed in public as it's one of their oldest and most closely guarded rituals. Juan Talegas (1891-1971) repeated the same superstition, adding that the *Alboreá* which is sung in public is not the same as the one Gypsies sing in private. It's hardly surprising their wedding ceremony should have become a secret ritual, since many of the anti-Gypsy laws forbade them from marrying, in a clumsy attempt to prevent them from having children.

But the mixing of fact and popular belief distorts the story to suit the argument, which is that Gypsies were so discriminated against, that they even had to celebrate weddings in secret. The famous Gypsy ceremony of "deflowering" the virgin bride, which no outsiders should witness, was originally a Castillian Spanish ceremony common throughout the countries of the southeastern Mediterranean. Even Queen Isabel de Braganza (1797- 1818) underwent this test upon her marriage to Fernando VII[89]. Among the Gypsies, it's performed by the older Gypsy women, one of whom introduces a white handkerchief into the vagina of the bride- to-be to break the hymen and then displays the blood-stained hanky as evidence of virginity. Here's a verse from a recorded Alboreá:

Ese pañuelito blanco	The white handkerchief
que amanece sin señal	Which has no mark
antes que amanezca el día	at the break of dawn
de rosas se ha de colmar	Must be filled with roses
En un verde prado	In a green pasture
tendiste el pañuelo	You laid out the handkerchief
salieron tres rosas	Three roses appeared
como tres luceros	Like three bright stars[90]

The verses of the Alboreá are in Castillian Spanish, with no Gypsy or Andalucían terms. The fact that it's sung in a chorus of voices, when all Gypsy cantes are supposedly solo, makes it doubtful that the Alboreá is originally a pure Gypsy cante. The chorus style is another characteristic of some Arabic-Andaluz song styles developed centuries ago.[91] In Morocco and elsewhere the nuba[92] songs sometimes use this kind of call and response singing, where one singer alternates with another, so it can't convincingly be claimed as a purely Gypsy cante.

---

[89]W. J. Fielding, *Curiosas Costumbres de Noviazgo y Matrimonio a Través de los Tiempos, La Prision General* 1965.
[90]*Lucero* refers precisely to the brightly shining planet Venus, It's common in flamenco terminology when referring to the beauty of a loved one.
[91]Christian Poché.
[92]A type of musical suite performed throughout Northern Africa.

THE DREGS OF SOCIETY

Gypsies weren't the only ones suffering from discrimination throughout all these royal pragmatics. During the reign of Isabel La Católica, Jews and Moslems were forced to convert to Catholicism or to leave Spanish territory where they had been established for hundreds of years. At the same time the infamous Gypsy edicts were enforced, outcast Moors were also living beyond the city walls of Granada and Sevilla. Most of the population were peasant farmers and labourers held in such disdain by the ruling classes that the aristocracy forbade *campesinos* (country dwellers) from coming into the limits of the court. In 1525 the Inquisitor in Jaén declared similar edicts for Arabs as those in force against Gypsies.

This verse from a soleá may have first been sung (but probably not in a flamenco voice) around this time, although officially the authority of the Spanish Inquisition lasted for several centuries:[93]

SOLEARES DE TRIANA[94]

Te quiero más que a Dios,	I love you more than I love God,
¿Jesús, que palabra he dicho	Jesus, what have I said?
Que yo merezco la inquisición	I deserve the inquisition

THE CRIME OF BEING GYPSY

The fact that the laws aimed at controlling Gypsies and their unsettling way of life were continually being revised and reissued for 300 years shows that they must have failed to provide the desired outcome; ridding the landscape of the pesky problem. And just what was their crime to begin with? Among the many legends relating to their origins are two which have held fast: It is said that Gypsy blacksmiths were ordered to make the nails used to crucify Jesus and that although they made four, only three were used. The fourth redhot nail is said to pursue them through the ages and that they're unable to escape it. A similar tale says a Gypsy blacksmith was ordered to make twelve nails to crucify three men, and he thought that the number 3 was a holy sign. So he hid one of the nails, believing that the man who was crucified with three rather than four nails would be blessed, and he would follow him for the rest of his days. In Serbia the Gypsies believe their ancestors stole the fourth nail from the cross and so they were condemned to wander for seven centuries. Another claim is that the original Gypsies were ordered to do penance for seven years by a Papal decree, and there is documentary evidence of such a Papal bull, only we can't be sure it's not a forgery.

Gypsies were accused of denying shelter to the Virgin Mary, of making a pact with the devil, of blasphemy, casting curses and of witchcraft, of treason, and of poisoning animal drinking troughs. They were even suspected of cannibalism. As recently as 1951, José Carlos de Luna[95] compared the habits of the Hungarian Gypsy with the Andalucian Gypsy and concluded that:

> *"There is something in which they are the same; dirtiness, as much from carelessness as from misery. You can say that of every thousand Gypsies, 999 are afraid of water....The Gypsy's brain is unlike that of any other race. Naturally hard and as fragile as glass? Clumsy and weak because he has not cultivated it?...Not even the most subtly ingenious will ever unwind that which they have wound up out of convenience or pure fancy...They say the Spanish Gypsy has the most base and perverted morals."*

[93] It was suspended in 1808, 1813-14 and 1820-1823 and finally abolished in 1834, having existed in various degrees of harshness
[94] Antonio Mairena: *Grandes Cantaores del Flamenco*, Phillips CD.
[95] Gitanos de la Bética- Gypsies of Andalucia- Betis was the name the Romans gave to the Guadalquivir River, and *Betica* was the province around it, roughly today's Andalucia. *Betis* is also the name of one of Seville's best known soccer teams!

The author does nothing to dispel these beliefs. Reading such statements, it's easy to recall the worst moments of scientific research, namely under the Nazi regime, and more recent attempts to prove that the brain of a homosexual is somehow less valid than any other, and predisposed to so-called aberrant sexual preference.

Despite all the stereotypes surrounding them, for example that they are pathological liars and have a natural ability to dramatize and embellish the simplest stories, the depth of suffering conveyed in flamenco, as their dramatic history shows, is based in fact. For three centuries, successive Spanish rulers issued laws against them which are often the only written evidence we have of their existence. If you add these historic facts to the basic social and cultural differences between Gypsy society and practically every other society, you can understand why they have a collective feeling of persecution and a perpetual sense of "otherness" which is still very much in evidence today.

THE ANDALUCIAN GYPSY

The Gypsies in Spain have always been considered a different branch of the Rom and Hungarian Gypsies. In Spain they call the Gypsies from Hungary and central Europe "Cingaros," the Rom's call non-Gypsies *gadjo*, the Spanish Gypsy calls non-Gypsies *gachó* and *payo*, and himself *gitano* and sometimes *calé*. In fact, there is no universal term among the Gypsies for their own race, but *gadjo* is the universal term for the non-Gypsy. Caló is the Gypsy word for 'black'. In Hindi and Punjabi the word is *kala*. The Andalucian Gypsy often has a striking resemblance to those we identify as Indians or Pakistanis, with rich black hair and eyes and dark skin. The words to many flamenco songs praise *la gente del bronce* (people with bronze skin). And they have always been known for their metalworking skills, perhaps left over from their days as warriors and sword bearers.

THE EUROPEAN GYPSIES

The nomads of central Europe, the Bohemians had spread out across Europe and Central Asia throughout the 15th Century, settling in different areas and gradually developing different lifestyles and habits. It's thought today that they are descended from three basic groups, or tribes: the Kalderash in the Balkans who are traditionally blacksmiths; the Gitanos (whom the French call Gitans) of Spain, southern France and parts of North Africa who are known as musicians and entertainers; and the Manush, also known as Sinti who are mostly in France, Alsace and Germany and who are often travelling showmen and circus people. Each of these groups is thought to have produced sub-groups according to their occupations or the country they originally came from. A century before the Gypsies came to Spain, there were already Gypsies in the Balkan countries, Cingarije were reported in Serbia in 1348 and in Zagreb and Corfu during the 14th Century.[96] Two Franciscan pilgrims to the Holy Land saw Gypsies living in caves in Crete in 1322, and from the Gypsy language comes the proof that they passed through Persia (modern day Iran), Turkey, Armenia, and Greece. In each of these countries the Gypsies speak their own variation of the Rom language but there are still many shared words.

The Spanish Gypsy dialect, *caló*, has added many words to the Spanish language, like *chungo*- ugly, or *chaval*, used commonly in Madrid to refer to a young man. In Rom a "young man" is *chavó*, in Sanskrit- *Chavale*, and in Hindi it's *chává*. The Armenian word for "horse" is *grá* or *graste*, Spanish Gypsies use the same word in Caló. The Turkish word for treasure - *mansín*, is also used in Caló. Slavic words such as *dosta* or *ulicha* are used with the same meaning in Caló ('enough' and 'street', respectively.) *Diquelar* is Caló for 'see', in Rom it's *dikh*, and in Sanskrit *diks*. The Gypsy word for pain or suffering is *duquela*, often sung in flamenco, which in Rom is *dukh*, and in Sanskrit *dukha*:

---

[96] J.P. Liégeois.

Yo le pido a Dios	I ask God
de que le alivie	To relieve my mother
a mi mare las ducucas	From the suffering
de su corazon	Of her heart

Las duquelas que tu tengas	The pains you have
bien merecías las tienes	You deserve them well
por tener tan mala lengua	For speaking so badly

In 1976 the Gypsy bailaor Mario Maya (b. 1937) produced his flamenco show *Camelamos Naquerar*, which is Caló for "We want to speak".

No me digas na	Don't say anything to me
Que me naqueras muy malamente	You speak badly of me
cuando tú te vas	When you leave

Camelar, often used in flamenco dialect, means "to want", "to love" or "hold dear":

Que yo no camelo eso	I don't want that
que yo camelo otra cosa	I want something else
que yo camelo un vestido	I want a dress
de color de rosa[97]	The colour of a pink rose

There are very few words of Arabic origin in Caló so it seems unlikely they were in Al-Andalus before the 15th Century.[98]

The Vlax Gypsies in Hungary came from Rumania where they had been used as slaves. They kept up the Rom language, and an ancient style of singing and dancing which has striking similarities with Spanish flamenco Gypsy seguiriyas and soleares.[99] In their *loki dili* style of slow song, the singer will abruptly stop singing halfway through a word, and then pick up again on the same vowel, which is also a mannerism in the seguiriyas and soleares. Modern day Pakistanis and Indians are always deeply struck by the similarities between flamenco singing styles and mannerisms and folk styles from their home towns. But similarities like these abound throughout the world. The traditional calls from the Japanese ringmaster during a Sumo wrestling ceremony sometimes sound like flamenco too!

Wherever they went, the European Gypsies have always been musicians and entertainers, often earning their small incomes this way. Their intuitive, natural musicality is the envy of most non-Gypsy musicians. In Spain, Gypsy street musicians still set themselves up on street corners, mostly with trumpets, accordions or ingeniously wheeled electronic keyboards. They play loud pasodobles,[100] always with great musical feeling, and sometimes accompanying a goat perched precariously on a stool. Once I noticed an old white car edging its way around a street corner in the center of Madrid with the trunk gaping open. Inside was the performing goat.

---

[97]Carmen Linares, *Mujeres en el cante* CD.
[98]Bernard Leblon, *Historia del Flamenco, Volume I*, Ediciones Tartessos.
[99]Bernard Leblon, *Gypsies & Flamenco*, University of Hertfordshire Press 1995.
[100]Traditional waltz-like two-step, always played ringside during bullfights and military parades.

Presumably they couldn't transport their star attraction on the bus. Spanish Gypsies probably picked up these tricks from the famous bear and animal trainers of the Gypsies of central Europe, Hungary and the old Yugoslavian territories. In the early 20th century a flamenco song style based on an old Andaluz folk song called the *Mariana* developed. It mentions the name Mariana in the chorus, which is supposedly the name of a monkey or a goat the wandering Gypsies trained to dance while accompanying it on the tambourine.[101]

THE GRAND ROUND-UP AND GENERAL IMPRISONMENT OF GYPSIES

King Carlos III (who ruled 1759-1788) is usually cited as the Gypsyies saviour after all the years of persecution. But his royal act of mercy in 1783 merely lifted the restrictions on trade and where they could live. The previous laws forbidding their dress style, language and way of life and forcing them to settle, were upheld. His brother King Fernando VI who ruled from 1746-1759, ordered the final solution to the 'Gypsy problem'. In 1749 all Gypsies were ordered to be simply rounded up and summarily imprisoned.[102] Over 12,000 Gypsies were imprisoned in the arsenals of La Carraca in San Fernando (Cádiz) and in the mines of Almadén, Cartagena and El Ferrol.

In the grand roundup prior to this general imprisonment, all those who were registered as Gypsies were literally carted off from their villages and homes to prison, and from there to forced labor in mines and in construction. In a 1974 article in the Cádiz newspaper, *Diario de Cádiz*, Luís Suárez Alvarez quotes a document which tells the story of 300 Gypsies who had been imprisoned in Seville and were taken from the prison there and shipped off to the naval arsenal of La Carraca in the bay of Cádiz:

"The population (who had gathered in multitude at the Plaza de San Francisco and around the prison) saw the farewells these men made to their wives, daughters and mothers and these to their menfolk, leaving them in charge of their children who were about six years old and upwards. And these men left the women in charge of the ones who were left, the little ones, and it moved everyone deeply. It was a shared feeling among all the population that they wanted to save these poor people and what upset everybody the most was the fact that they didn't know where they were being taken, and that they were being separated in the knowledge that they might never see one another again. The prison that afternoon was a form of hell, with the Gypsies shouting and crying from the railings the same as when they said goodbye as well as afterwards. The same thing happened later in the prison of La Hermandad when that night they took the prisoners from there and took them to the river by torchlight; and it was certainly very painful to see these families because there was no pity nor shelter to be found in the whole kingdom."[103]

THE GYPSY, THE FLAMENCO AND THE ANDALUZ

Government censors were sent to every community to record who lived where and who held what profession so they could determine where Gypsies were making it easier for the authorities to round them up. Since the majority of the Andalucian population were illiterate, it's possible the censors would write down the Gypsies' names and professions for them, categorizing every member of the community. The result might have been something like; 'Miguel Heredia, butcher; Gypsy.' Gypsies have always lived side by side with the rest of the population, often working in jobs which were indispensable in rural communities despite the laws which

---

[101]Jose Blas Vega, notes for CD *Maestros Clasicos del Cante,* Sonifolk 20156.
[102]La Prision General, Antonio Zoido.
[103]Idem.

forbade them from anything other than farming. They worked as butchers, sheep shearers, horse dealers and farriers, basket weavers, blacksmiths and farm laborers. Considering these jobs were mostly illegal for them, they must have escaped the laws with the help of their non-Gypsy neighbours. How else can we explain the fact that most villages throughout Andalucia had Gypsy populations, although they were only officially allowed to live in four distinct places? Rounding up and carting off Gypsies caused a lot of problems, since it meant depriving towns and cities all over Andalucia of many essential services. In 1749, how could rural life have continued without a blacksmith, or sheep shearers, grape pickers, olive pickers, butchers, or bakers?

The confusion of *lo gitano*, *lo flamenco* and *lo Andaluz* (that which is Gypsy, flamenco or from Andalucia) seems to have existed for as long as history can recall. In Andalucía today, just as it must have been in past centuries, Gypsies are not the only people who hold traditionally Gypsy jobs. The ordinary 'indigenous' Andalucian also works on farms, picking olives and fruit, clearing land, sheep shearing and goat herding, picking grapes to collect in the woven baskets which Gypsies also traditionally made, and selling meat. Some of these jobs were considered exclusively Gypsy, so if you were a horse trader or basket weaver, a butcher or farm worker, you were probably thought of as Gypsy whether you were or not. Many of these trades mean periods of travel, just to get to the crops, for example. So there has always been a tradition of "roaming" workers in Andalucia. When the order to round-up and imprison Gypsies came, some local authorities refused to hand over their Gypsy neighbours. Already in 1746 officials in Jerez had intervened to allow the Monge family to remain in the city where they worked as blacksmiths. In Vélez Málaga, fifteen Gypsy families were allowed to remain because they were alleged to be *Castellanos Viejos*–Old Castillian Spanish–a term which was used to describe settled Gypsies, and dates from the time of the Arab settlement when it also referred to indigenous Spaniards.

Even today and in flamenco's recent past, there are performers who held so-called Gypsy trades before turning professional. For example: the non-Gypsy guitarist Pepe Martínez (1923-1984) was a butcher by trade, until he became a professional performer. El Cabrero (b. 1944), a popular non- Gypsy cantaor from a village outside Seville, was literally a goat herd, as his professional name implies. Agujetas de Jerez was a blacksmith before he turned professional, and he still turns his hand to the anvil once in a while.[104]

According to documents of the time of the General Imprisonment, the Gypsy population in Andalucia was the most numerous in Spain, mostly in and around Seville and the Atlantic port of Cádiz. 'Los Puertos'- the ports, refers to the Puerto de Santa María and Puerto Real, cities not far from Cádiz. Antonio Mairena sings about the Gypsies from these areas in this *cante por toná*,[105] which may refer to this little episode of 'ethnic cleansing'. These verses show that the scars run deep, and the memory is kept alive in the traditional lyrics to songs like this (on following page):

---

[104]*Agujetas Cantaor*, film by Dominique Abel, 2000.
[105]Sung without guitar accompaniment, but with the syllabic rhythm of a seguiriya.

SEGUIRIYA DE LOS PUERTOS

Los gitanitos del puerto,	The Gypsies of The Ports
fueron los más desgraciados.	Were the most unfortunate.
Y en las minas del azogue,	To the mercury mines,
Se los llevaban sentenciados	They were taken, under arrest,
Y al dia siguiente,	And the next day,
les pusieron una gorra,	They were made to wear hats
y alpargata de esparto,	And slippers made of sparta grass
Y del sentimiento ahogado	And in sorrow they drowned,
Y pa' dale más martirio	And to make them suffer even more,
les pusieron un maestro,	They gave them a master
Que el no daba alivio.	Who never let them rest.
A palos, a palitos	Beaten with sticks, with sticks,
los dejaban muerto.	They were left for dead.[106]

MERELY GYPSIES....

So the experience of imprisonment and suffering family separations, confiscation of property, and forced labour is a shared one in the history of Andalucians, both Gypsies and payos. Those who were imprisoned (the law was upheld for 17 years), had all their belongings confiscated and sold and their families were divided, so by the time they were released there was nowhere and nothing to go back to. During the general imprisonment many Gypsies were released to return to nothing. No homes, no savings, no jobs, no family and a society in decadence, leaving them practically no choice but to turn to crime for survival. Is it any wonder they became known as petty thieves and criminals, given the conditions they had to endure?

In 1762, a year before Carlos III ruled that all Gypsies should be freed, the commissioner in the Royal Arsenal of El Ferrol (in the northern state of Galicia) wrote complaining about 67 prisoners held there who were: "old, useless and worn out, completely incapable of any work," of these, 43 prisoners names were cited, beside them were the words: *meramente gitanos* - merely Gypsies.

Government officials began taking notice, and asked other naval and army bases for data about the prisoners they held. From Cartagena the prisoners wrote: *"in that year, in 1749 at one o'clock and two o'clock at night, we were taken prisoner, women and children, all those to be found in the Catholic reign of Spain, to become servants of our Lord and King... The same thing happened after in the prison of La Hermandad when that night they took the prisoners from there and took them to the river by torch light; and it was certainly very painful to see these families because thtere was no pity no shelter to be found in the whole kingdom."*[107]

Flamenco exists nowhere else, and arose nowhere else but the specific areas of Andalucia, Extremadura and Murcia where there were large Gypsy populations. The other common thread between these areas, is that imprisoned Gypsies after the general round-up, were sent here to work in forced labour, or simply held until they could be shipped off to parts of the empire in South America, or to the mines in the north of Spain. Or to work as slaves in the galleys, and in construction of many of the monuments and buildings one can still see across the country. Knowing all this, it's easier to understand why ordinary Andalucians as well as Andalucian Gypsies are capable of singing a blood curdling cry of pain in flamenco.

---

[106]*Grandes Cantaores del Flamenco*, Philips CD522 086-2.
[107]*La Prision General Antoinio Zoido.*

CHAPTER 8: ARE THEY IMPROVISING?

"In flamenco everything has been prepared."

Paco de Lucía

"You have to know where you are, and not know where you're going to be in 15 seconds."[108]

On his first tour with jazz guitarists John McLaughlin and Al di Meola in 1980, Paco de Lucía suffered headaches and backaches from the tension of not knowing how to improvise alongside his stage companions. But once he'd figured it out, he found he couldn't do without it.

So what does *improvisation* mean? Strictly speaking, it means to make it up as you go along, but making it up as you go along, without any grounding in the basics and no sense of structure would produce a mess. In music just as in any other art, you can only improvise on a given structure. You can't improvise successfully or meaningfully without a sense of basic structure. Although it seems each flamenco singer, dancer or guitarist may be improvising, in fact they are sticking to the guidelines of flamenco forms which were laid down centuries ago.

Flamenco is a supremely individualistic art, performed with all manner of personal embellishments which is what makes it look improvised. Performers are spontaneous. Spontaneity isn't the same as improvising from thin air, and every flamenco performer has a repertoire, a collection of styles they can draw from spontaneously. Does that mean flamenco is performed without rehearsals, without discussing what key it's in or who's going to sing and who is going to dance? Yes, except in the stylised theater presentations by artists such as Joaquín Cortes or Sara Baras. Generally, a cantaor will decide which *palos* to present to the public, and discuss with his guitarist what version he'll sing. The Tangos del Titi, or Malagueñas del Mellizo, for example, two styles named after the cantaores who originally sang them. In informal flamenco gatherings, people already know the forms well enough to just launch into them, safe in the knowledge that everybody else knows what key that *palo* is in. And they all follow the patterns laid down centuries ago.

The cycle of the *compás* is always maintained. Within the *compás* the guitar often plays repeated phrases called *llamadas*–a call, which are like musical mannerisms that indicate a different section of the song or dance. The *llamada* announces a *falseta*–a melodic interlude–in other words, a quick tune from the guitar player, or a singer's next phrase, or a dancer's *escobilla* - a section of the dance when the footwork becomes the focus. These moments are the same in every *soleá, alegrías seguiriya* or *tientos*, in fact in every palo *a compás*- style with a strict rhythmic cycle. So the musical pattern is not improvised, although it's elastic in the sense that there's no set 'four bar intro'. It might turn out to be a six bar intro if the singer is taking a swig from a drink, or just isn't ready to open up.
The guitarist Manolo Sanlúcar said:

> *The essence of flamenco was built years ago, in our generation little has been contributed as*
> *far as forms go: seguiriyas, soleá, malagueñas, taranta, granaína, tangos, bulerias and all the*
> *others exist from way back. We take these forms and give them a new turn, enrich them harmon-*
> *ically, invent new melodies and so on but we don't create forms. The styles are done.*[109]

Flamenco is something you have to live in order to catch the subtle signs that something is about to begin or end. Just like when you go out with a group of people in Spain and nobody has decided where you're going, you can end up standing on a street corner for half an hour or more, while everybody discusses whether to go to this bar or that, and in between times a couple of conversations might start up. Even when somebody

---
[108]Video Light & Shade.
[109]*Acoustic Guitar Magazine*, Article by Guillermo Juan Christie March April 1995.

says: "Okay, let's go." They won't necessarily make a move, until some subtle change happens, and then they'll start to drift off. For outsiders this can be incredibly frustrating, as there's no way to explain what that subtle sign is, it's just something in the air. Flamenco is the same.

Unlike classical musicians who prepare to play at a certain time and in a certain way, Flamencos can just turn up and play. If it's a big dance production which has been rehearsed, then everything has to start in a certain way and on a certain note. But a cantaor and tocaor, will often get together for the first time in the changing room (if they are lucky enough to have one), decide what songs they'll start with and maybe warm up a bit. The guitarist Andrés Batista recalls an example of this free style when he was asked to accompany the great bailaora Carmen Amaya:[110]

> We were in the changing rooms when the dancer La Morita asked me to go through the Garrotín so she could go over the words. A couple of minutes, if that, went by and Carmen who was in the next room putting on her makeup, came in and said: 'I didn't know you knew the Garrotín! I'll perform it tonight.' And she went back to her dressing room. I was dumbfounded because the Garrotín doesn't have any set moves for the dancer, it seemed risky to me to perform it in public without a rehearsal.(...) When I started playing the introduction I was on maximum alert because I didn't know where she was going to make her entrance from, nor what dance she would do. Carmen emerged like a queen in her white 'bata de cola', moving with incredible majesty and at first with a measured pace, which little by little gathered a dizzying rhythm which lead to a series of turns and movements with the 'bata de cola' which drew a unanimous ovation from the public. Her words, sung with interludes from the guitar, and answered by zapateados, her postures, escobillados etc. gradually described a clear choreography of rhythmic filigrees, movements and picaresque expressions (typical of this style) which fortunately my playing synchronised with perfectly, uniting with her dance in a mutual feeling, which allowed us to guess or intuit what each other was about to do before we did it. The performance was a great success and Carmen, after obliging me to take the curtain alone several times, came up to me and gave me a kiss on the cheek and said, 'that's the way to play Andrés!'

Each interpreter is expected to add their own dimension, their own rhythm of breathing and their own sense of the words to each palo they sing. Each rendition of a *seguiriya*, a *soleá*, *tientos* or *martinete*, is a recreation of that palo or form, in the unique style of the performer. Never a copy, but a version. Sometimes a performer or interpreter will come along with such a strong character, who makes such a notable contribution to the interpretation of a style, that their names become associated with it. Therefore you'll get versions of the Malagueñas de Chacón or of El Mellizo the Tangos del Titi, the Fandangos de Juan Breva, the Tarantas de Fernando el de Triana, Granaínas de Frasquito Hierbabuena etc. which are all named after the singer who perfected them in his own style.

The Gypsy singer Antonio Mairena (1909-1983) was another powerful personality, creating a 'school' of singing known as *Mairenismo*. The Gypsy singer Fernanda de Utrera (b. 1923) is another, her renditions of the *soleá* having become so highly regarded as to be known as the *soleá de Fernanda*. El Camarón de-la Isla (1950-1992) has had such an impact on flamenco that today all young singers–both male and female–have been influenced by his style, which is known as 'Camaronero', or 'Camaronismo.' Enrique Morente has also been a huge influence on the next generation of singers and guitarists. Guitarists also take phrases and falsetas from singers, and vice versa. The guitarist Pepe Habichuela said that Morente sang a snippet of his own

---

[110]"My Time with the Wonderful Carmen Amaya" *Flamenco International* magazine Vol 2 N° 4

soleá.[111] The guitarist Paco Cortes, Carmen Linares' usual accompanist, confessed he uses musical phrases and ornaments of Enrique's: *"Yes, I have some variations on Enrique's cante, I nearly always remember his style and I play them."* Morente also influenced El Camarón de La Isla in whose voice one can hear Morentian phrases on recordings such as the tangos on the live CD 'Camarón Nuestro' recorded in 1978 and 1979. José Mercé has also been known to reproduce Morentian falsetas.

Antonio Mairena also declared that: *"El Cante is already created, what you can't do is create anything new, it's all been prepared."*[112] He would listen to old cantaores and pick up bits and pieces of songs and snatches of melody from acquaintances, and let them brew in his head until he was ready to play around with them and give them form. In this way, he 'recreated' the *Giliana*, a cante he based on the soleá form and which is related to the old Romances. The *Giliana* is rumoured to have been sung by members of Enrique El Mellizo's (1848-1906) family and was perhaps the basis for the name which is often quoted as the first known flamenco singer Tío Luís El de La Juliana. No reliable data exists about this figure, and so the Juliana he was presumably named after is sometimes thought to be either a place, or his mother's name. But the Caló word *'gillabar'* stemming from the Rom and Hindu languages meaning to sing, may be the origin of the word Giliana or Jiliana as in a type of song. It's easy to see how Giliana could become Juliana. Originally Tío Luís's name may have been Uncle Luís the Singer.

Mairena used his flamenco instinct to recreate many songs and made a big impression on flamenco because of this. It's impossible to know just how much of his 'recreations' were actually pure invention, and how much can really be considered salvaging an old form from extinction. Either way, his enormous talent and musicality has left a legacy which enriched flamenco when it was going through the Opera Flamenca stage of its history.[113]

The themes of the songs have been passed on from one generation to another, and in this way flamenco is a culture rooted in traditions, any one who ignores them or tries to change these, is always criticised. The challenge is to *recreate* with a personality and artistry rooted in experience and tradition. But most of all, it's in the flamenco ambience that singers learn the words and styles of *palos*, adding their own twists and turns to make them their own. Since flamenco isn't written down, but learned by ear, it's more open to little changes and personal decorations- embellishments- than formally composed music.

Today young singers can study digitally enhanced recordings of past masters to learn their technique. Many of today's up-and-coming stars take a rather studious approach to their performances and present a polished programme which is almost as well-rehearsed as a classical concert. These recitals don't feel spontaneous, but more like an effort to prove they are *cantaores largos*; singers who can manage all the different song styles.

As Camarón said when asked about improvisation:

That's the hardest thing. I try to do a cante which is modern and ancient at the same time. That sounds steeped in tradition yet is of the moment. I like improvising, but for that you have to study the old Gypsies a lot, get to know their songs inside out. The only way to advance towards being able to improvise is to study the old guys. I've spent my life studying the cantes of Torre, Mojama, el Gloria, La Repompa, Chiquito de Camas, Alfonso de Gaspar, Manolito Maeía, Juan Talega, José de Paula, el Chozas. Nobody remembers most of them.[114]

---

[111]Enrique Morente, "La Voz Libre", B. Gutiérrez SGAE 1992.
[112]A.A.Caballero: "El Cante flamenco", Alianza Editorial 1994.
[113]See Chapter 9, "What's The History?"
[114]Interview in *El Europeo*.

IS THE MUSIC WRITTEN DOWN?

El cante is difficult to write on the five lines of the musical stave, because the rhythm of the vocal line doesn't always fit within the same bar lines as the guitar part, and because of its 'improvisational' feel. You can count the uneven five beats in a *seguiriyas* on the guitar for example, but the singer elongates and distorts the syllables of the words, and splits them intuitively in a way which is practically impossible to write down accurately. Almost every vowel sung in *el cante*, is distorted. To the traditional words the singer may add *ayes*, adding his or her own feeling for the traditional *letras*, or phrases like *madrecita de mi alma* -sweet mother of my soul. Except for the theme of each individual cante, which is always the same, the verses are 'improvised' in the moment, drawing from a huge collection which has been passed on from one generation to the next.

Flamencos like to draw a difference between themselves and a classical musician, whom they think is restricted by the notes on the page and all sorts of rules for interpretation. But they're not so different, since the forms and lyrics in flamenco have been in existence for centuries, and even individual interpretations are 'copied' from one generation to the next. The same arguments for purity exist in both camps. In the world of classical music, there is a desire to be 'authentic' by playing Bach or Beethoven exactly as they would have heard it, on instruments from their day. In flamenco, innovators are criticised for adding new instruments and harmonies to the ancient forms. Overlooking the fact that it's impossible to know how a performer interpreted a particular song 200 years ago, purists are like anti-evolutionists, seeking some sort of ideal for which we have no recordings.

Sometimes you may get the feeling there are only so many verses of flamenco available for singers to use. In a week long festival of various cantaores, on one night I heard three: Rancapino, Dieguito El Cigala and Juan Moneo "El Torta", sing the same verse of alegrías:

Con la luz del cigarro	By the light of my cigarette,
yo vi el camino,	I saw the path,
El cigarro se apagó,	The cigarette went out,
perdí el camino	And I lost the way

Here's an example to show the degree of 'improvisation' in the cante:
Camarón de La Isla sings these 'letras por Tarantos'[115]:

Las vueltas que el mundo da,	The way the world turns,
válgame Dios tío Rufino	Lord preserve me, Uncle Rufino
siendo un minero tan fino	Being such a fine miner
adónde tú has venío a parar	Where have you come to rest
a darle vueltas al molino	Providing the windmill its turns

---

[115]*El Camarón de la Isla con la colaboración especial de Paco de Lucía*, PHILIPS CD 848 539-2.

Ines Bacan[116] sings the same lyrics 'por tarantos', but with these personal variations;

Las güertas que er mundo da,
!várgame, tio Rufino,
las güertas que er mundo da!
Siendo un minero tan fino
dónde ha venío a pará, ay, y ay! ...
a darle güerta a un molino.[117]

---

[116]*Soledad Sonora*, CD Ethnic B6873.
[117]This lyric illustrates how the tarantos form is always about mining.

CHAPTER 9: GROWING PAINS, FLAMENCO'S ADOLESCENCE
What's the history?

Flamenco is only in its adolescence. Imagine writing the biography of a fifteen-year-old, and you'll get an idea of the confusion surrounding it. In its formative years it wasn't very good at explaining itself and its behaviour was often erratic. As it developed, it started mixing with some very unlikely elements, often causing an uproar in the neighbourhood, but made itself very popular. At the moment, just like most adolescents, flamenco is making new friends, experimenting with strange substances, trying on new clothes and staying up late.

The study of flamenco is rather undisciplined, which means a lot of theories have taken hold by virtue of repetition, not because they have been thoroughly researched, nor for their proven scientific value. Only in the past generation has flamenco gained acceptance as a high art, and therefore become worthy of serious study. The term *flamencología*- flamencology- the science of flamenco, was coined after the book *Flamencología* by Anselmo González Climent was published in 1955. During the 1800's and early decades of the 1900's practically none of the writers on flamenco had any experience of it as musicians or performers, and Flamencos quite rightly felt they were being judged by people unqualified to pass judgment. Although someone may be born an artist, nobody is born a flamencologist. The late, great Camarón de La Isla coined the term *flamencólicos,* a play on the word *cólico* (which has the same meaning as in English), to defend himself against the Flamencólogos who claimed he was ruining el cante: *"I'm not interested in what the flamencólicos say. I go about my business and they go about theirs, although it seems they can't stop talking about what I do."*[118]

SILENT HISTORY

We can only trace flamenco back to the late 1800's, not before. The style of singing, the melismas and chromaticism, modes and rhythms, and all the ornamentation that we hear in el cante flamenco both today and in the earliest recordings have existed for centuries. But not as the flamenco forms we know today, since it takes more than just these elements to make something flamenco.[119] A little research reinforces the very un-academic assumption that everything we see and hear around us is the result of centuries of borrowing, mixing, adulterating, altering and copying each other, whether in language, music or behavior–in a word, 'culture', which is rarely isolated and arguably never 'pure'. Unravelling the various influences and origins of something like flamenco can enhance our understanding of certain aspects, but it probably won't make much difference to our appreciation of it in the end!

We can only follow flamenco's development from the anecdotes and accounts of Flamencos who were involved in professional performing, none of whom were 'trained' musicians, able to decipher the confusion of modes and keys and write them down, none of whom were historians eager to record the developments surrounding every performance. It is easy for us to forget that not every cantaor or cantaora was recorded. The history of flamenco is filled with artists, professional or amateur, whose voices can not be digitally enhanced for us to judge and add to our pantheon of flamenco legends. Since the dawn of recording, we have written the history of various musics according to a who's who of recording which ignores the influence of hundreds of unrecorded voices.[120]

---

[118]Francisco Riva interview, *El Europeo*, Nº 33, June 1991.
[119]See Chapter 1, "What Is Flamenco?"
[120]See Chapter 4, "Flamenco's Founding Fathers".

Besides relying on the accounts of those whose careers led them to a recording studio or concert tour, we can investigate flamenco's musical roots, which are shared by Spanish and even Portuguese regional folk music, and therefore don't offer any explanation as to how come flamenco developed at all. The same influences affected other Spanish composers and musicians, such as Alonso Mudarra (1510-1580), Manuel de Falla (1876-1946) or Joaquin Rodrigo (1901-1998). It's very hard to establish a relationship between styles of music that are separated by several hundred years, because our hindsight is clouded by all that has happened since. Flamenco, like almost everything else in Spanish culture and in other countries, is the result of a mixture of many different elements. It may be the first true fusion in the history of music.[121] In the words of the Californian composer Lou Harrison *"Don't underestimate hybrid music BECAUSE THAT'S ALL THERE IS."*[122]

PRE-FLAMENCO POETRY

During the 12th and 13th centuries, the troubadours who sang in the language known as Langue D'Oc–from Occitain, the region comprising southern France and extending to parts of Italy which spoke the language–roamed most of Spain, and were often popular court musicians. The Provençal language, still spoken today, is a dialect of the Oc language and a surprising number of words in flamenco and Spanish generally have their origin in Provençal. Debate rages in academic circles as to the influence of Provençal poetry on Spanish vernacular verse and whether Arabic poetry influenced this, or vice versa. There are many similarities between the Provençal, Arabic and Spanish Romance styles: syllabic metre and subjects being the most obvious. In 1928 the Spanish academic Julián Ribera suggested the Provençal word *trobar* from which the word Troubadour stems, may have its roots in the Arabic *taraba* - to sing or play music, to be moved by joy or grief, or to fill with delight.[123] The troubadours left a remarkable legacy in literature and song, with the same themes popping up in flamenco today, and in popular verse and song. The words of this song are attributed to the Troubadour Raimbaud de Vaqueiras, they are strikingly similar to a flamenco theme:

Tanto he perdido mi saber,	I have lost so much knowledge
que apenas sé donde estoy.	That I hardly know where I am
No sé de donde vengo,	I don't know where I've come from,
ni a donde voy,	Nor where I'm going
ni de qué valen el día	Nor what the day, and being
y el ser	Is worth
Estoy en tal estado,	I'm in such a state
que ni velo,	That I can't be awake
ni puedo dormir.	Nor can I sleep
No me place vivir, ni morir,	Not life nor death pleases me
ni el mal ni el bien me importan.	Neither good nor bad, is important to me.[124]

---

[121]See Chapter 13, "What is Flamenco Fusion?"
[122]Lou Harrison's *Music Primer*.
[123]"Arab Influences on European Love Poetry." Roger Boase, *The Legacy of Muslim Spain, Vol.1*.
[124]CD, *Trovadores Catalanes y Provenzales*, Hispavox.

THE GOSPEL ACCORDING TO....

The origins of flamenco no doubt lie in the musical history of Spain, but most of all in the history of the people who live and breathe and sing and dance flamenco. There's an abundance of conflicting theories about how the singing style developed. For Antonio Machado Y Álvarez *Demófilo*, the author of the first would-be scientific study of flamenco, the early stage was a hermetic period when it was supposedly only performed by Gypsies behind closed doors, kept secret from society. *Demófilo* believed that flamenco originates with a Gypsy style of singing, but he never explained what this was, apart from claiming that the *soleá* and *seguiriyas*, *tonás* and *polos* embodied it. Nevertheless, his theory has been the basis for most subsequent investigations, which may be why there are so many different explanations and opinions about flamenco's history. If you start by assuming flamenco comes from something which you can't clearly define and combine it with the emergence from a secretive, hermetic period we can't possibly know anything about, then the rest of your explanations are bound to be complicated.

The Gypsies have been in Spain since before the 15th century, but flamenco only began to develop when the laws controlling their lives began to soften three hundred years later, in the 1780's. Perhaps because of this three hundred year gap in flamenco's history, Antonio Mairena, (1909-1983) supported Demófilo's theory (without acknowledging him) in his book *Mundo Y Formas Del Cante Flamenco*, which has become flamenco dogma. Apparently, once flamenco emerged from this so-called hermetic period, it gradually changed and adapted according to the desires of the non-Gypsy audience.[125]

The theory follows that original Gypsy ritual songs and dances, perhaps accompanying events like the slaughtering of a pig, or celebration of a wedding or a birth, have been taken out of their social context and changed and adapted to become entertainment for an audience. But it seems odd that a culture so rooted in traditions and customs such as the Gypsy society, should modernise its musical rituals and not the rest of its social system. Gypsies to this day maintain a traditional and secretive life-style. It seems more likely that the Andalucian, always attracted to the Gypsy's ways, copied *them* in performance and song, producing a unique style we call flamenco, based on Gypsies but developed by payos.

Following on from Mairena's dogma only the *seguiriya* and *soleá* are now considered pure cantes. But even these supposedly untouchable styles have gone through transformations and alterations, as we can tell by listening to recently released remastered old recordings from the early 1900s. The existence of an original Gypsy Cante which composers Manuel De Falla and Joaquin Turina mentioned without describing, has never been proven. Rather than talk about a mysterious and indefinable Gypsy Cante, it makes more sense to talk of a Gypsy *interpretation* or manner of singing which is how all flamenco singers try to sing. The French Gypsyologist J.P. Liégeois wrote about it like this: *"Gypsy culture is based on indescribable and intangible ways of being and doing things which abide by their customs and laws. Their way of doing things is part of their way of being and the only important thing about the ritual is the ritual itself."*[126] Therefore, there's no such thing as a Gypsy song but a Gypsy *way* of singing.

AFRICAN FLAMENCO

Recent research has shown the powerful influence of native African rhythms and dances on Spanish Folklore, particularly flamenco.[127] In 1565 Seville had the second largest population of African slaves in Europe, Lisbon in Portugal holds ignominious first place. These slaves would gather to perform their dances,

---

[125]See Chapter 7, "What's The Gypsy's Story?"

[126]J.P. Liégeois "Gypsies, An Illustrated History", Al Saqi Books, London 1986.

[127]"Semillas de Ebano," J.L Navarro García Portada, Editorial Biblioteca Flamenca N°4 1998.

either as entertainment or simply spontaneously as an expression of self identity and as part of their religious beliefs[128], and their movements became so popular that theater and dance groups adopted them, as the abundance of popular lyrics from theatre productions of the 16-17th Century show.[129] The *tango* and *zorongo* originally date from this period, although the changes the different dance steps went through in order to reach us today as the flamenco bailes we know are not traceable. It is even possible the fandango, considered such a fundamentally Spanish Folk form originated with the dances of the Blacks. As early as 1464 the term *fandangueros* was used in Jerez to describe the noisy, animated gatherings Black and white slaves used to organise.

AL-ANDALUS

The Arabs invaded Spain in 711 B.C. The Catholic monarchs expelled them from Granada, their last stronghold, in 1492 although this didn't represent the complete expulsion of Moors from Spanish soil. The Moorish king Boabdil was allowed exile in the Alpujarras[130] mountains, but after just a year he was forced to leave the country and the Moorish population left behind were forbidden from carrying out their traditional customs and way of life. A rebellion against the Christians began in the region in 1568 which lasted for two years, after which the Muslims were exiled to the northern regions of Spain until 1614 when the official decree of expulsion arrived.

Altogether that's a thousand years of cultural influence. The abundance of Arabic names across Spain and in particular the Andalucian region is part of their legacy and shows how deeply Spain's history is affected by the Arabic or Islamic influence. An estimated 20% of the names of rivers and villages all over Spain, are originally Arabic[131]: Qurtuba, Talabira, al- Mariyya, al-Jazira al-Khadra for example are now called Cordoba, Talavera, Almería and Algeciras. The name of the river which runs through Andalucía and unites most of the flamenco areas, the Guadalquivir, is the Spanish adaptation of the Arabic for 'Great River'. In the Spanish language (Castillian Spanish) there are approximately 900 originally Arabic words in constant use. Like 'artichoke'- *alcachofa*; 'rent' -*alquiler*; 'olive'- *aceituna*; carrot -*zanahoria*; canal- *acequia*-, not to mention the everyday expression *ojalá* which stems directly from the Arabic *insh'alla*; God willing.

Flamenco has a lot in common with an Arabic style of singing. The Arabic, or Moorish influence within flamenco is easy to see and hear, but it doesn't by itself explain why this form of music sprang up in Andalucia, hundreds of years after the Moors were forced to leave, and not further north, in Zaragoza for example, where the Arab culture was equally well established. The old Mozarabic territory which extended north beyond Andalucia as far as Zaragoza, is called al-Andalus. Here, a unique style of music developed called Arabigo-andaluz, and there are many similarities between this style of music and flamenco. Like the highly ornamented vocal style and details such as how the words are actually sung. Despite the fact that the history of Arabigo-andaluz music is quite well documented, tracing the style itself of early Moorish music in Al-Andalus, for example–how it was sung and what modes were used–is extremely complicated since none of it has survived in written notation. Like flamenco, it was never written down but passed on orally.

[128]The zarabanda originated as a dance to the bantu goddess of the same name
[129]Semillas de Ebano, J. L. Navarro García Portada, Editorial Biblioteca Flamenca N°4 1998
[130]*South From Granada*. Gerald Brenan, Hamish Hamilton 1957.
[131]Dieter Messner: "Arabic Words in Ibero-Romance Languages" *The Legacy of Muslim Spain, Vol 1.*

ARABIGO-ANDALUZ TONGUE TWISTERS

Arabigo-andaluz singing style favours the clarity of syllables over melismas (singing one vowel through several different notes), and the balance between poetry and musical content has always been fundamental in Arabic music. The addition of extra syllables which don't mean anything is also common, just like in flamenco[132] and some of these are exactly the same in flamenco today. Called *taratin* (in Byzantine times the term was *teretismo*), these extra syllables are sung in the poems of Arabigo-andaluz music today, but unlike flamenco music, in Arabigo-andaluz styles they're only added in certain places with a special significance. Like *ha-na-na* for example, or *ya-la-la-li* which is almost exactly what La Paquera de Jerez often opens one of her powerful bulerías with: *Ay-li-li-li.* But extra syllables are common in all types of vocal music around the world.

Two unique forms of Arabic poetry were developed in Al-Andalus: the *muwashaha* and *zajal*. Both of these were specifically for singing, not just recitation. The muwashaha are thought to have been invented in Spain in the 10th Century by Muqaddam ibn Mu'afa de Qabra, known today as *El Ciego de Cabra* (The Blind One of Cabra). The word *muwashaha* means "embroider", a highly ornate style just like the very ornamented style of flamenco singing. The music to these poems wasn't written down, only the mode (musical key) and the rhythm. This was enough to trigger the memory into remembering the rest. The muwashaha developed a particular ending called the *kharja* (also spelt *jarcha*). The *jarcha* were unique to Al-Andalus music, these were short verses sung to finish off the *muwashaha,* composed in an old Ibero-Romance dialect called Mozarabic[133]. Many *jarcha* are similar to verses in today's flamenco.

Take a look at this line from a *jarcha*:

a mibi non queris

sin el habib non vivreyu.

That *mibi* is the same as the habit in flamenco singing called *babeo* which is when the singer elaborates a word using extra sounds of 'bo bo' or 'bi bi', like this word sung by Antonio Mairena: *periquito,* which he repeats, adding a babeo:

Periquito peri bibi bi quito

Fernanda de Utrera uses the *babeo* a lot in her soleares, for example finishing off the word 'careful' in the Andaluz dialect- *cuidaito-* in this way makes it become:

Que cuidaito-bo-bo

SOCIAL HISTORY

Around the time when flamenco was developing, Spain was going through all sorts of cultural and social changes. In the late 1700s and early 1800s the Romantic movement in Europe was flourishing and Spain, rather than participating or contributing to the movement, inspired it. Romanticism was the fashion to glorify everything in nature, and popular or common traditions and customs. For the English and Germans, where Romanticism began, Spain, with its Muslim history and the stories of heroism from the time of the French occupation became the quintessential 'romantic' country, and all things Spanish became fashionable. According to historians, the country's immersion in the Romantic literary movement didn't start until 1834, and before this it was theater and stage productions glorifying the popular or Folkloric which dominated the cultural scene.

---

[132]See Chapter 6, "What are they singing about?"
[133]"Zajal and Muwashaha." James T. Monroe, *The Legacy of Muslim Spain, Vol 1.*

GITANISMO

Since the 1780s a stylised form of 'gipsiness'- *Gitanismo* was becoming fashionable. In the late 1700s and mid 1800s the middle classes and working classes began adopting the mannerisms and dress styles of Gypsies, most likely prompted by the innumerable theater productions which used stereotypical characters drawn from the vast underworld of the margins of Spanish society. 'Gypsy' became fashionable as a label, *lo agitanado* was all the rage in theatres and social gatherings. Even today most non-Gypsy Flamencos adopt a Gypsy style of clothing, hairstyle, speech and mannerisms. Even well educated intellectuals within flamenco will affect a slang speech and bad grammar, just to play the role better. The fashion for all things Gypsy meant that paradoxically, this shunned sector of society became a model for ordinary Andalucians to copy. It's practically impossible to define the reasons for a fashion taking hold. Why did platform shoes become popular? What made wearing dark sunglasses indoors fashionable? Why is it fashionable to wear trousers with the crotch around your knees? Like the eternal problem of the rebellious adolescent, it's cool to be 'bad' now, and it probably always has been and always will be.

POLITICS AND WAR

The Spanish War of Independence began with Napoleon Bonaparte's invasion of Spain in 1808. He was forced to retreat in 1813, with the help of foreign allies, the Duke of Wellington among them. The country underwent a profound soul searching after the war, seeking an identity untainted by foreign influences, eventually giving rise to 'costumbrismo,' Spain's version of Romanticism. *Costumbrismo* is the origin of most of the stereotypes about Spanish culture which are still in place today, both within the country and elsewhere. But really that should be all things *Andalucian*. Like the *mantilla*, the guitar, castanets, fans, the style of layered dress known as *faralaes* worn today during the spring fair of Seville and still called a *traje Gitana*-Gypsy dress- and always associated with flamenco bailaoras, earrings and ornaments in the hair, the trappings of bullfighting, and anything to do with horses have all come to represent Andalucía. To this day, these elements represent Spain generally in the minds of most people, although they all stem from one specific region. Even within Spain, many people reject what they call this stereotyped image, the *españolada* . We should remember that bullfighting is banned in Barcelona for example, and that the folk music of Galicia and the Basque Country sells more CDs than flamenco.

Politically, Spain was divided between supporters of the old king, Fernando VII and revolutionary liberals led by Colonel Riego who even established their own constitution in Cádiz in 1812, the first in the history of Europe. Riego was later executed after leading an uprising in Las Cabezas de San Juan outside Seville in 1820. Silverio Franconetti[134] first sang of this event in 1865 in a seguiriyas which became known as the seguidillas[135] 'De Riego':

Matáron a Riego	They killed Riego
ya Riego murió	Riego is dead now
como se viste, se viste de luto	How we dressed, we dressed in mourning
toa la nasión	The whole nation

---

[134]Silverio Rey de los Cantaores. J. Blas Vega Ediciones, La Posada 1995.
[135]During this time the names of many flamenco forms were not fixed as we know them today.

It looks like this event is also recounted in this *seguiriyas*, sung by Antonio Mairena in 1973:

SEGUIRIYAS DE LOS PUERTOS[136]

No lo permitais	Don't allow
Que los Franceses	the French
que están en la Isla	who are on the isle,
no se metan en Cádiz	to enter Cádiz.
Salgan canastitos de San Juan	Bring out the little baskets of St. John
de Dios para pedir limosna	to beg for alms,
para el entierro	for the funeral
de Riego	of Riego.
que válgame por Dios	May God save me

Between 1825 and 1833 Sevilla was governed by the brother of one of Bonaparte's advisers, Jose Manuel Arjona, who organised the Semana Santa (Holy Week) celebrations into the parades of holy figures we see today. He also founded the school of bullfighting -Escuela de Tauromáqia de Sevilla, which saw the start of a new style of *corrida* where the matador stands up to receive the bull, rather than sitting on a wicker chair which was how the corridas were conducted up until then. Bullfighting has always been associated with flamenco because it was normal for bullfighters and their assistants (the *cuadro* made up of *mozos de espada*, *banderilleros* and hangers on) to celebrate after corridas in the 18th Century equivalent of night clubs, where they mingled with flamenco dancers, singers and entertainers. The two *aficiónes* flamenco and bullfighting date from the same period, they share the same jargon and similar artistic values, and since the 1800s have often been united by marriages between bullfighters and flamenco singers and dancers. The most recent union of flamenco and bullfighting came with the marriage of Estrella Morente, Enrique Morente's cantaora daughter, to the matador Javier Conde in 2001.

FLAMENCO WITH A DOUBLE LATTE- The Café Cantante

When evaluating the different periods of flamenco, flamencologists have tried to divide the time line into conveniently identifiable eras, just like classical music historians naming different musical periods. The stages flamenco has passed through until the present day are identified by the venues where it was staged, as well as the artists who were most popular at any given moment. The best documented period begins with the establishment of the Café Cantantes, when flamenco was first organised as a public attraction and staged in 'cafes' where artists were paid to perform. This period lasted from the 1890s to the 1920s during which there were nearly eighty cafés registered in Spain, mostly in Andalucia and Madrid. The café cantantes existed from around 1846, but flamenco was not part of the entertainment offered until the last decade of the 1800s.[137] One of the most famous cafés was run by Silverio Franconetti[138], an Italo-Spanish flamenco singer and therefore a non-Gypsy. Demófilo used to frequent Silverio's café and published a biography of him at the end of his collection of flamenco verses "Colección de Cantes Flamencos". Ironically, Silverio seems to represent everything Demófilo disapproved of: he commercialised flamenco, professionalised it and brought it out of the

---

[136]*Todo el Flamenco* CD de la Seguiriya y la Soleá, Edilibro S.L. 1998.
[137]Sociología del Cante Flamenco, G. Steingress, Centro Andaluz de Flamenco Jerez 1991.
[138]See Chapter 4, "Flamenco's Founding Fathers".

taverns and secretive back rooms of private reunions where Demófilo felt it belonged. Yet Demófilo considered him to be one of the best *cantadores* of Spain, specialising precisely in those Gypsy styles he declared best represented el cante jondo.

The café cantantes were extraordinary venues where almost anything went on, including bull baiting, if there was room! In 1898 Robert B. Cunninghame Graham published a description of a scene in the Salon Ojeda of Seville, known more popularly as el Café del Burrero:

> *This temple of the dance was a huge building, broken down like a grain storage room, dusty, with an air of desolation emphasised by the oil candles hanging on the walls. In the middle of the sandy floor, around wooden tables the cream of Spanish playboy society sat on rickety wicker chairs while standing along the walls were groups of men who, judging from their clothing could only be pimps and horse traders, all with very greasy hair combed forwards onto their foreheads in a fringe, tight trousers, short buttoned jackets and felt cowboy's hats with stiff rims which they would run their fingers along every so often to make sure they were straight.*

In the cafés, the main attraction was *el baile*–the dance. During this early period of flamenco it was el baile which set the stage. Cunninghame Graham goes on to describe the sorry looking appearance of the performers lined up on stage, the musicians to one side:

> "*Two guitarists and other players of a small instrument they call a bandurria which is like a cross between a guitar and a mandolin and is played in a peculiar way, at first monotonous but then little by little, like the beat of a drum, ending up making the audience's blood boil, imposing a silence and attracting all eyes to the stage. The rasgueo of the guitars was never ending. This is produced by passing the hand across all the strings at once and has something of the mysterious noise made by turkeys when they drag their wings across the floor.*"

He goes on to describe el cante:

> "*Suddenly, one of the men broke out in an almost wild song, with such strange intervals and oscillating beat and confusing rhythm that at first it seemed to be the cry of a wolf rather than a song, but little by little its strangeness penetrated the soul and moved one to the marrow. He who has heard this music finds anything else afterwards is tasteless and boring.*"[139]

OPERA FLAMENCA

The café cantante era saw the rise of many of flamenco's legendary figures who indelibly influenced the art and subsequent artists up until the present day.[140] Artists such as don Antonio Chacón, La Niña de Los Peines and Manuel Torres began earning a living performing in these venues, causing subsequent historians to name the era as a Golden Age. Gradually the cafe cantante gave way to a more theatrical presentation of flamenco in travelling variety shows dubbed *Opera Flamenca*. The term Opera arose in 1924 when the impresario Carlos Hernández, alias Vedrines, started touring with large companies following the format of a popular variety style show. He called his productions Opera Flamenca to avoid paying the higher tax which was levied on smaller theatre productions. The shows had nothing to do with opera in the classical sense, as they were not mounted productions including stage back-drops and a script. This style came in five years later when playwrights Quintero and Guillen produced their stage show *Opera Flamenca*. The same star artists who earned their living in the café cantantes moved with the times and worked in Opera Flamenca.

---

[139]La Serneta Nº 1, 2000.
[140]See Chapter 4, "Flamenco's Founding Fathers".

The Opera Flamenca period has been described by many as the most dreadful, artless and degrading period in flamenco history. One of its most virulent critics Anselmo González Climent who coined the term *flamencology*, wrote that the Opera Flamenca period established the lighter styles such as *fandangos, farrucas, garrotín, zambra, alegrías* and *bulerías* as the public's idea of flamenco. He said: "Consequently, there's no understanding of the 'cante grande' (*seguiriyas, soleares, martinete...*)." It's interesting to note how the constant evolution of flamenco and aficionados has given the bulerías and fandangos such pride of place in today's family of flamenco forms, just 40 years after this criticism was written.

Most of the best known names of the period took part in the Opera Flamenca era including Carmen Amaya, Ramón Montoya, Manuel Torre, Los Chavalillos de Sevilla (Antonio and Rosario), Vallejo and Angelillo. During this period Pepe Marchena created a lyrical style of *fandango* with melodramatic lyrics and mannerisms, and a staged theatricality, which was so popular that it became known as Marchenismo. Many of the dramatic gestures so common in flamenco presentations today probably date from this time, when cantaores had to hold the attention of a crowd in bull rings and cavernous theatres with no microphones.

THE 1922 CONCURSO DE CANTE JONDO

Flamencologists always cite the 1922 Concurso de Cante Jondo organised in Granada as a landmark occasion in the art's history, possibly because it represents one of the few times intellectuals and established artists from other fields paid flamenco any attention. In 1922, the composer Manuel de Falla considered the Gypsy cantes to be the essence of Andalucian Folklore, and 'Flamenco' was for him the watered down and popularised version of it. Along with the poet Federico García Lorca and their friends, writers, poets and playwrights as well as classical composers and musicians (including the famous classical guitarist Andrés Segovia who was a member of the jury) they determined the flamenco forms which would be admitted in competition: *seguiriyas, martinetes, carceleras, cañas, polos saetas* and *soleares*.

The organisers Falla, Miguel Ceron, and a 22-year-old García Lorca believed it was professionals who were about to bring the art of cante jondo to its ruin, and so professionals were banned from participating. As the writer José Luis Ortiz Nuevo, founder of Seville's world renowned flamenco festival the Bienal de Sevilla remarked: "What kind of arrogance assumed that those who performed for a fee were incapable of transmitting the true depth and grandeur of el cante jondo, when every one of the competition's organisers were themselves professionals in their field?" In the event, La Niña de Los Peines and Manuel Torres were invited guests, and Chacón presided over the jury. It seems professionals had their role to play despite Falla's disapproval of *fandangos, tangos, bulerías* and *alegrías,* which each of these artists performed daily.

One of the winners was a young Manolo Ortega 'Caracol' (1909-1973) who went on to become one of the revered figures of flamenco's history. At the time he was just twelve years old and he shared the prize with Diego Bermúdez 'El Tenazas' (1850-1923) who was seventy-two. The success of the competition is difficult to assess. The organisers had hoped and planned to found schools of cante jondo where youngsters could go and learn from the old maestros, presumably to maintain the art, just like the concept of a classical music conservatory which does exactly as it says: it conserves. The young Manolo Caracol may have proved a disappointment to Falla since, rather than avoid professional venues and keep to private reunions, he immediately returned to Seville where he appeared in the Reina Victoria theater alongside El Tenazas. Without the hard work of professionals, where would flamenco be today? Still stuck in taverns and back rooms, shared among a privileged few who declare themselves the only true guardians of a forgotten art which would bear no relevance at all to modern society.

NACIONAL FLAMENQUISMO AND TABLAOS

The Opera Flamenca period lasted through the 1950s, although there are no concrete events defining its end. From the 1940s through the 50s flamenco was presented as a national art by Franco's artless regime. This style of presentation has been dubbed *Nacional flamenquismo,* a nationalisation of flamenco which continued to present its more entertaining facet, accompanied by continued repression of the Gypsy culture and outright denial that this minority ever had anything to do with it. Mairena's extreme assertions may owe a lot to this constant official repression and denial. He was looking for formal recognition that his race had contributed something worthwhile to Spain by attributing the most highly prized aspects of flamenco to Gypsies alone.

Every stage in flamenco's history is ambivalent. During the hated Opera Flamenca period some of the best artists performed, yet flamenco was cheapened and lost its dignity. *Nacional flamenquismo* gave rise to every cliché you can think of connected with flamenco, from women in spotted dresses with flowers behind their ears to the image of the Spanish macho male. Yet artists such as Caracol, Bernardo el de los Lobitos, Fernanda and Bernarda de Utrera or La Perla de Cádiz thrived in the tablaos founded during this time. Flamenco's enigmas and contradictions continued.

The tablaos could be considered the natural progression of the café cantante, incorporating the theatrical presentations which became fashionable during the Opera Flamenca period. The Tablao–from *tabla,* –meaning plank as in a stage- is really the 20th Century equivalent of the original Café Cantante. A cross between restaurant, cabaret and night club, tablaos consist of formally presented flamenco shows which are generally staged at the end of a meal. Most tablaos have a bar area and restaurant style floor space with a stage at one end, and for a fixed price offer three course meals, wine and flamenco show. Often criticised for presenting 'flamenco for tourists' the tablaos have fallen into disrepute, and today the well known tablaos in Madrid are in a period of decadence, with artists giving automatic performances. In the early days the tablaos were often the breeding ground for emerging stars and considered the graduation school which one had to pass through. Tablaos provided the bread and butter for such established performers as El Sordera de Jerez, Terremoto, La Paquera, or Manolo Caracol who owned his own tablao, Los Canasteros. Even modern artists such as Camarón or Enrique Morente worked in tablaos such as Zambra, Café de Chinitas and Torres Bermejas. Such artists cut their teeth in the daily routine of two performances a night.

The tablaos have been almost as criticised as the Opera Flamenca by flamencologists who maintain that The Real Thing can only be experienced in Andalucian back waters with a select audience of 'enteraos'- those who understand. It seems to be the same argument against professionalism that Demófilo voiced in 1881- a hundred and twenty years ago! The assumption is that presenting flamenco as a planned series of bailes and cantes, with artists dressed appropriately for a theatrical performance, with staged lighting and amplification robs it of its flamencura. Many times this is true, and in most tablaos on any given day of the week tourists witness a kind of shallow representation of flamenco, with performers who don't fully involve themselves in their performance. Experience and cynicism has proven to them that the audience is content (although they never actually ask them) with a display of the expected clichés- some fast foot work, sensuous gestures, staged emotion from the cantaor and adequate guitar accompaniment. Nevertheless, since the beginnings of professional flamenco so-called tourists have been a major part of the audience and to assume that artists in tablaos 'dumb down' their flamencura for foreigners is offensive for both audience and artists. Many people who visit the tablaos get their first taste of flamenco here, for better or worse, and are compelled to go and buy a recording, or see a more established artist's theater production. Little by little, their afición grows and thus the tablao is not a wholly negligible nor bad aspect of the modern flamenco scene.

Since the 1950s with the appearance of books like Mairena and Molina's *Mundo Y Formas*, Gonzalez Climent's *Flamencología* and the first recorded anthology of flamenco cante[141], the art has been under continual reevaluation. The flamenco generation of the 1970s were soon dubbed Los Nuevos Flamencos- The New Flamencos- with Nuevo Flamenco becoming the umbrella term covering all kinds of experiments.[142] More competitions were organised, more festivals established and more *peñas* opened, local clubs where aficionados gather to hear each other and invited guests.

[141]*Antología del Cante Flamenco*, Hispavox
[142]See Chapter 15, "What Is Flamenco Nuevo?"

CHAPTER 10: FLAMENCO GUITAR OR SPANISH GUITAR?

"The Spanish guitar" has come to be the name for all guitars made using the Spanish method or design of construction. But this doesn't mean all Spanish guitars are flamenco guitars, or even made in Spain. You can play practically any style of music on a nylon strung 'Spanish' guitar. It's not the instrument which makes the music classical or flamenco, but the technique and the approach of the player.

The guitar as we know it is only as old as flamenco. Although all sorts of instruments very similar to it existed as far back as the Medieval ages, they were not the same size, or made in the same way. There was no standard guitar. The instrument called the *guitarra*, which the English called the *gittern*, emerged around the mid 1550s. The lowest sounding string on this guitar was called a *bordón*. In Argentina, Paraguay and Uruguay, they still use this word to describe those strings with the deepest sound, perhaps a word left over from the original Spanish settlers who introduced the instrument to South America in the 16th Century. The term is still used in flamenco, but not so much in classical guitar. The early or baroque guitar gradually evolved into an instrument more like we are used to today. Although it was smaller and tuned to a different pitch, this guitar had six double courses of strings until the 1830's when the single six string guitar began to gain in popularity. Most of the formal music published for the baroque guitar was influenced by French and Italian schools of composition; accompaniment to popular songs and dances wasn't published. Today, if you listen to the music composed for the baroque guitar played on replicas of the originals, you can easily hear how the flamenco guitar technique has absorbed both these plucking and strumming techniques.

GUITARRA MORISCA AND GUITARRA LATINA

The early guitar was mostly used to accompany popular songs and dances, so the overriding technique was strumming. The two types of guitar mentioned in writings from the day took their names from the techniques used to play them. The *guitarra morisca* was mostly plucked with the fingers or a plectrum and the *guitarra latina*, or *castellana* (also called the *guitarra rasgueada*,) was strummed. For example the works of the best known composers for guitar in those days Santiago de Murcia (c.1680-c.1740) or Gaspar Sanz (c.1645-c.1715) often take their inspiration from popular tunes and dances like the *fandangos* and *canarios*, blending energetic rhythmic strumming with single-voice melodies. The *fandango* dance in 3/4 time already existed in the 16th Century; it's one of the oldest folk forms in Spain and the popular *fandangos* of Andalucia- more properly *Folkloric fandangos* - have gradually been assimilated into flamenco. The styles grouped under the heading De Levante (the East) are derived from regional fandangos: the Malagueñas are the flamenco fandangos from Málaga, the tarantas is the flamenco fandango from Almería (there is a regional non-flamenco dance called simply the Fandango de Almería). The fandangos from the province of Huelva consist of 33 different styles, with 10 regional variations, including the Fandangos De Alosno which includes 16 variations and where the fandangos are considered to originate, the fandangos de Lucena, de Calaña, de Huelva, de Andévalo and so on.

The classical guitarists Fernando Sor (1778-1839) and Dionisio Aguado (1784-1849) composed many charming works for the solo guitar as well as songs and chamber pieces, which are all standards in the repertoire today. But none of them have a particularly Spanish character. It wasn't until they each gave in to popular demand and composed their own *fandangos* that they published music using the *rasgueos* and rhythms we associate with Spanish popular music, and particularly with flamenco. The last movement of the classically constructed *Fantasie Opus 54* for two guitars by Fernando Sor is called *Allegro dans le Genre Espagnole* -an

Allegro in the Spanish style. Aguado composed his *Variatons on the Fandango* in 1835 which, after years of formal compositions in the standard European style, suddenly shows a very Spanish character.

Aguado had taken lessons as a child near Madrid from a well known guitarist called Padre Basilio who was particularly famous for his *fandangos* in the 1780s and 90s. The Italian composer Luigi Boccherini wrote a famous quintet in the style of a *fandango* he had heard played by Padre Basilio: the *Quintettino imitando il fandango che suona sulla chitarra il Padre Basilio* -"Quintet which imitates the fandango played by Padre Basilio." Later it was arranged for guitar and strings and today it's one of the best known works for guitarists. Both Aguado's and Boccherini's composition share the same melody, so maybe Aguado remembered a tune he used to hear his old teacher play when he was a student, and adapted it to the formal structure of a theme and variations.

CASANOVA'S FANDANGO

The popular Fandango of the 1700s had such a lascivious nature that even Casanova was shocked by the sensuality of the couples dancing it. Casanova wrote his memoirs in 1768 and talked about his impressions of the dance he'd seen performed by couples in a masked ball. He was told at the time that he should see it danced by Gypsies if he wanted to get the real thing:

> *"It's impossible to describe, each couple, man and woman, never taking more than three steps at a time and playing castanets to the sound of the orchestra, make a thousand movements, take up a thousand attitudes with a lasciviousness with which nothing can compare. There is found in it the expression of love from its beginning to its end, from the sigh of desire to the ecstasy of possession. After dancing such a dance it seemed impossible to me that a woman could refuse anything to her partner, for the fandango carries within it all of the arousals of voluptuousness."*

THE ANDALUCIAN GUITAR

The modern six stringed guitar developed early in the early 1800s, and it was precisely in Andalucia, where the best luthiers or *guitarreros* were to be found. Curiously, the cities which had large Gypsy populations, Cádiz, Sevilla, Granada and Málaga had the largest number of guitar makers.[143] Presumably because they had quite a lot of customers needing instruments. Between 1847-1920 there were approximately 80 Café Cantantes- where flamenco was performed regularly- across Spain: 32 in Sevilla and 15 in Madrid alone, which would have had at least four guitarists each, working every night. By 1833 the guitar was so popular, that there were fifteen guitar makers recorded in Madrid for a population of only 200,000.

The Andalucian guitar makers introduced construction innovations which still influence the way the guitar is made to this day. The use of fan strutting, came from the Sevillian maker Francisco Sanguino during the early 1800s. These are thin strips of wood stuck in a fan design under the soundboard, which reinforce the lower bout (below the sound hole). Josef Benedid of Cádiz (who was active between 1760-1836) was one of the first to experiment with fan bracing, and it's thought he taught one of the most famous makers of his day, José Pagés, who along with his brother Juan, was working in Cádiz between 1794-1819. Josef (also known as José) Martínez of Málaga, Manuel Muñoa and Juan Moreno in Madrid also used the fan bracing design. One of the earliest known flamenco singers, El Planeta, is known to have used a guitar made by José Martínez of Málaga, as recorded in a scene in the famous book *Escenas Andaluzas* by Estébanez Calderón:

---

[143]"Cultural Origins of the Modern Guitar", by Richard E. Bruné. GFA *Soundboard* magazine, Fall 1997.

"This character of great standing, judging from his clothes and by the deference granted him by those around, carried under his arm, with a relaxed air of courtesy, a beautiful vihuela one didn't need to hear in order to deduce that it was the product of Málaga and legitimate daughter of those skilled and intelligent hands of the famous and aging maker Martínez. This guitar was wide in the bass and marvelously delineated in its cut, the neck drew attention because of its gracious style, the little bridge was of ebony as were the frets, the pegs with their little holes were the colour of pomegranate and the head was of Ivory, from which the hooks for hanging it up hung on white and red ribbons. The instrument was in fact an entire orchestra, by that I mean it had six strings which were very fine, with rich bordones *of silver."*[144]

LA GUITARRA DE TABLAO

Antonio Torres (1817-1892) the guitar maker from Almería, founded the modern construction of the guitar as we know it today, in both its *classical* and *flamenco* design. He didn't have a different approach to making classical or flamenco guitars; he used the same method of construction for both types. Up until 1839, crafts guilds laid down strict rules which governed the guitar making profession. Anybody wishing to set themselves up as a guitar maker had to abide by these, which included exams and apprenticeship, which makes it sound like a thoroughly professional occupation. But apart from a high standard of woodwork or craftsmanship, the few surviving instruments from this period show that neither the makers nor players had much idea about the tone qualities of different woods. Throughout the 1770s and up until 1850, until Torres standardised some of the measurements, the guitar was made in different sizes and with different construction techniques from one maker to another. There was no set pattern to abide by, and even the types of woods varied enormously, as though luthiers didn't realise the importance of the different tone qualities of each species; guitars were made from practically any type of wood with a straight grain.

Only in the mid 1800s did the construction of the flamenco guitar begin to differ from the construction of a classical guitar and this was basically in the type of wood used. The flamenco guitar was called the *guitarra de tablao* -the stage guitar- with a slightly arched, or domed soundboard. They were usually made of spruce, pine or sometimes cypress, because these woods were cheap and readily available. But for the backs and sides, just about anything went. The differences between the construction of the two types of guitar have come about because of the techniques used to play them. As in all art, theory and technique follows practice. In other words, first comes the art, and then comes the explanation of how it's done.

Because the flamenco guitar had to be heard above the accompaniment of a dancer's feet, a singer, *jaleos* and *palmas*, so it was constructed to have a more percussive and penetrating sound. Today, the flamenco guitar is lighter in construction than a classical guitar, the body is slightly smaller with a thinner top, or soundboard. The fret board is often narrower than a classical guitar, and the strings marginally closer together and closer to the finger board, and consequently to the soundboard. Which all makes it easier to play. Some flamenco guitarists joke about the height of the strings above the top of the classical guitar, called the *action*, saying they could put their sandwich under the strings. And not just any old sandwich, but a thick *bocadillo de tortilla*- a potato omelette sandwich.

THE MADRID MAKERS

Spaniards Fernando Sor and Dionisio Aguado were both using small-bodied guitars made in either Spain or France during the 1800s. Dionisio Aguado played Muñoa's larger guitars and Sor recommended the

---

[144]"Escenas Andaluzas" Serafín Estébanez Calderón, 1847.

Benedid, Martínez and Pagés instruments. Today, master guitar maker José Romanillos, who is also Antonio Torres' biographer, believes Aguado's influence over the Muñoa makers, urging them to produce a "modern instrument with single strings", was the turning point for the modern concert guitar in Spain. The Madrid school of guitar making established in the late 1800s by Manuel Ramírez, dates from the period of Aguado's influence over the Muñoa brothers, between 1800-1826. In his guitar method *Escuela de Guitarra* published in 1825, there's a drawing of Aguado playing a guitar probably made by Juan Muñoa, which looks similar to the larger guitars that Antonio Torres eventually developed.[145] Players must have had quite an influence on guitar makers as they still do, and it's logical to assume flamenco players, who must have outnumbered classical players during these years, knew the kind of sound they were looking for in an instrument and demanded it of the makers.

Although it's likely flamenco guitarists couldn't afford a top rate instrument, and cypress was often used because it was cheap, it has become the preferred wood of both flamenco luthiers and players. The traditional peg -head style of attaching the strings to the head of the guitar on wooden pegs rather than mechanical string winders, is simply a left over from the vihuela and lute construction and also makes the instrument lighter. It's interesting how the construction of the flamenco guitar has sprung from the need to keep the instrument both cheap and light, yet has also ended up giving the guitar the sound qualities which are most sought after by today's players. The establishment of two separate construction techniques for the flamenco guitars and the classical was completed by the Madrid luthiers Santos Hernández (1873-1942), Domingo Esteso (1882-1937), and Marcelo Barbero (1904-1955).[146]

WHAT'S THE DIFFERENCE BETWEEN FLAMENCO AND CLASSICAL PLAYING?

The guitar is technically one of the hardest instruments to play well, because it's so versatile. It is at once a harmonic, melodic *and* a percussive instrument. You can play polyphonic music on the guitar; i.e a singing melody with an accompaniment at the same time, or you can play single voice melodies like a flute or violin, or you can strum chord shapes in interesting harmonisations. And you can do all three at once, which although is also true of other instruments like the piano, on the guitar you only have one hand to do it with, both the melody and accompaniment: the right hand.

The right hand is the most important in both classical and flamenco playing, since it's responsible for the actual sound you hear. The left hand only governs the pitch of strings and a few 'tricks,' but by itself doesn't produce music. All guitarists have to develop speed, strength and stamina in the right hand. The modern flamenco style involves a very complex right hand technique combining a fine muscular control involving both the back of the hand and the palm of the hand. The typical flamenco *rasgueo* (a strum across all the strings) uses the muscles and tendons of the back of the hand to send the fingers down and away from the palm and strings, whereas nearly all the right hand techniques for the classical guitarist draw the fingers of the hand in towards the palm, very rarely sending them outwards. The classical guitar uses almost no rasgueos. Solo flamenco performers have to dominate both the *rasgueo* technique as well as the straightforward plucking, when the fingers come in towards the palm of the hand.

---

[145]*Antonio de Torres Guitar Maker- His Life & Work.* J. L. Romanillos. Element Books, Ltd.
[146]Idem.

THE SCRATCH AND TAP

The *rasgeuo*[147] of the flamenco guitar is one of the unmistakable characteristics of the music; each flamenco form has distinct pivotal points consisting of these rasgueos in the particular key or sequence peculiar to that form. The soleá is the most obvious example, and is used to teach beginners because it contains the basis for many other palos. The chords of the rasgueos give the basic harmonic/modal character of the song and in between these, the guitarist can play melodic interludes, a *falseta*. That word may comes from *falsear* which means to falsify, or deform something, which is perhaps what cantaores thought guitarists were doing when they began filling in the moments of a song where the voice was quiet. But the Andaluz habit of deforming words themselves makes one wonder whether this is not simply a regional pronunciation of the word *fraseta*- a short phrase- which the Andaluz dialect would be prone to turn into *farseta*- hence *falseta*.

The flamenco guitarist also has to be able to tap the top of the guitar, usually with the ring finger to make the unique *golpe* sound which marks the rhythm and silences, and accentuates moments in the *compás*. The characteristic tap plate which is stuck on the top of the flamenco guitar just under the sound hole, is to protect the thin wood from the *golpe*. It's likely the *golpe* developed to help both dancer and guitarist determine where the beat fell, or more interestingly, the space between beats. And as with all other things connected with flamenco, it's been so highly developed that it's more often seen as an ornament than an aid to performance. The well-known French Gypsy guitarist Manitas de Plata abuses the golpe technique using it indiscriminately, instead of according to the demands of the compás. He's one of those who has made a name for himself outside the Spanish flamenco world where these sorts of techniques are not always understood in the context of the music, but simply seen as impressive effects. The flamenco guitarist's right hand thumb is also far more acrobatic than in classical guitar playing, producing notes by using both a downstroke and an up stroke, a technique called *alzapúa* - literally 'raising the pick'- which is unique to flamenco.

THE TRIPLE APPRENTICESHIP

Traditionally flamenco guitarists should undergo an apprenticeship, learning to accompany *el baile*, and *el cante* before developing their creativity as soloists. The dance accompaniment is the most demanding physically because you literally have to sit and repeat over and over the same compás while the dancers learn their steps. The concert flamenco guitar's string tension is very similar to a classical guitar, which is what causes the stress and strain on the right hand, constantly repeating rasgueados. This means the hand repeats the same muscle and tendon movements over and over, which is the cause of tendonitis.

The student flamenco guitarist builds stamina and endurance, and gains a solid grounding in rhythm by accompanying dance classes. Accompanying singers is more musically demanding. This is where all flamenco comes from, and singers often behave as though they are the sole guardians of the secrets of flamenco, and treat novice guitarists with disdain. The young guitarist from Barcelona, Chicuelo, remembered his early apprenticeship accompanying singers at his local peñas[148]:

> *"You never know who's going to sing what. At any given moment there could be 5 or 10 singers and you have to accompany each one of them, and they all ask you for a different style. Are you going to get hold of the genealogy of flamenco to see what they're singing, maybe 50 song types? Well, you have to know each one of them. Lots of times I learned the hard way, at first they'd ask me for things I didn't know, but that makes you go and learn. By the following week I knew what that was and how to accompany it."*

[147]Believed to stem from the verb *rasgar*- "to scratch."
[148]*Alma Cien* magazine N° 21.

According to Paco de Lucía:

"In order to be a good flamenco soloist you have to know the art in depth, and therefore complete several stages. One of them, which I consider fundamental, is learning to accompany both el cante and el baile. This takes many years, but it's what gives you mastery over the basis of flamenco. From there, with what you could call this traditional baggage, you can allow yourself the luxury of playing as a soloist. He who tries to start off as a soloist will always be handicapped. In el cante you'll find all the language you need to become a soloist–a meaningful soloist because, no matter how brilliant the music he can play and however clean his technique, if it doesn't smell of Andalucía and have that sense of the ancestry, he'll be a good professional, but he won't be playing flamenco."[149]

Often, people assume a musician's hands and fingers are strong, like a weight lifter. They mistake stamina for strength. Think of the long distance runner, who is usually thin and wiry, not a strong looking physique at all! The long distance runner is the closest in athletics to the musician whose hands are very finely attuned to the tiny muscular movements involved and which have to be sustained and repeated over and over again. I've often witnessed members of a *cuadro*[150] massage their hands and shake their arms as though trying to relieve the tension that builds up after sustained performance. The problem of tendonitis and focal dystonia among guitarists and musicians generally is very common. Focal dystonia is basically a repetitive strain syndrome which causes the tendon of a finger to literally seize up. The brain loses control over it. In the worst cases it can force a player to quit altogether since the only solution is complete and prolonged rest, although the classical player David Leisner[151] has successfully retrained his neural pathways to return to concert performing. It would appear Perico el del Lunar suffered this complaint. According to J. M. Gamboa his biographer his prodigious facility was gradually eroded *"by a progressive paralysis in the ring and little finger of his right hand (...) Pericon de Cádiz*[152] *used to joke that it looked like he was playing with a handful of hazelnuts. Perico had to reinvent his technique, which was limited in arpeggios and tremolos, but he never lost an ounce of his depth and effectiveness."*[153]

FLAMENCO VS CLASSICAL

The history of the flamenco guitar is as plagued with shadows as the general history of flamenco. Only recently have investigators begun to uncover the extent of exchanges between classical players and their flamenco counterparts, gradually laying to rest the traditional animosity between the two schools. Andrés Segovia (1892-1987) has perhaps done more to create and cultivate the perceived rivalry between classical and flamenco guitarists than any other guitarist. Segovia began playing the guitar in the flamenco style, in those days more often referred to as *folkloric*. Somewhere along the line he decided to dig a ditch between himself and flamencos. This despite having sat on the jury of the famous 1922 flamenco competition held in Granada, organised by his friends Manuel de Falla and Federico García Lorca, and having himself given a recital on the opening night during which he played soleares. During the mid 1800s the best known 'classical' guitarist, Julian Arcas (1832-1882) played both folkloric pieces and his own formally composed works. It is rumoured he taught Miguel Borrull (1866-1926) who is credited with composing the Rondeña form for solo flamenco guitar and who performed both flamenco forms and classical pieces, although the latter it is said, only in private.

---

[149]Interview Ronda Iberia in flight magazine J.M Velázquez-Gaztelu July 1994.
[150]The traditional name for the flamenco lineup of singer, guitarists and dancer.
[151]Professor at Manhattan School of Music
[152]1901-1980
[153]Perico el del Lunar, *Un flamenco de Antología*, La Posada 2001.

In 1885 Paco el Barbero (1840-1910) also performed the works of Arcas and Verdi alongside tangos, soleares and peteneras. Guitar players during the early years of flamenco were more versatile than we are today, with our unfortunate tendency to consider "pure" only that which is limited to a single style. In the late 19th Century and early 1900s the guitar shop of Santos Hernández was a meeting spot for guitarists of all types. The famous flamenco guitarist Ramón Montoya heard the classical guitarist Miguel Llobet there, and it's said he incorporated the techniques and sounds he heard Llobet performing into his own playing thus enriching flamenco guitar technique. Ramon Montoya (1880-1949) and Manolo de Huelva (1892-1976) both incorporated classical guitar techniques into their flamenco playing.

It's worth noting that Luís Maravilla was the first flamenco guitarist to perform the emblematic concerto for classical guitar by Rodrigo; *The Concerto de Aranjuez* in Barcelona in 1952. Rodrigo sent an autographed photo of himself with a note of personal thanks and congratulations to Maravilla, a conveniently forgotten fact by 1992 when Paco de Lucía recorded and performed the concerto in the composer's presence. An interpretation which Rodrigo qualified as 'folkloric', but which went on to outsell all previously recorded versions.

"PLUCK, PLUCK, PLUCK–THAT'S NOT TECHNIQUE"

The flamenco guitar has undergone an extraordinary development during the past 50 years with countless young guitarists emerging with dazzling technique. Curiously, the same thing has happened in the classical guitar world, where more and more youngsters are blessed with a natural ability for the difficulties of the guitar. Playing fast scales and dominating the instrument technically is now normal in both classical and flamenco guitar. In 1971 Diego Del Gastor, an icon among aficionados of the flamenco guitar, was asked the difference between the guitar in his time, and 50 years previously, he replied that, *"Today it's played much faster, and players dominate the guitar."*[154] But he also made clear that dominating the instrument isn't the same thing as good quality musicianship. This is true for both classical and flamenco performers whose technique and virtuosity aren't always matched by an interesting musical personality.

A lot of music for classical guitar has more lyrical and complex voicing than most flamenco music, as well as melodic lines which should be sustained like a vocal line. This is a problem for classical guitar players because the sound of the plucked string dies away so quickly; the guitar naturally has very little sustain. The sound of the plucked guitar string is produced immediately; there's no gentle buildup similar to what you can achieve by a drawing a bow across the strings of a violin or cello. Neither is there a lingering aftertone as with the piano whose notes will die away only if you physically lift your fingers from the keys and your feet from the pedals. In effect, the plucked note begins to die as soon as you hear it. In the words of one of the greatest classical guitarists, Julian Bream, *"Every time you play a note there is a decay and your whole life is spent resuscitating decay."*[155] Classical guitar luthiers are always working to give the instrument better sustain and more volume, its evolving design has given it a more rounded tone, a bigger volume and longer sustain. The flamenco guitarist doesn't have to worry so much about sustain because flamenco is generally more percussive and increasingly harmonic than melodic. For the past 50 years or so, solo flamenco guitarists have been using a guitar whose construction combines the elements of a classical guitar with those of a flamenco guitar; the bright percussiveness with a richer sounding bass and better volume. The backs and sides of these guitars are often made of rosewood, a dark red wood often used in constructing a classical guitar. A flamenco guitar with rosewood back and sides is known as a *flamenca negra*- a black flamenco guitar.

[154]*Rito y Geografía del Toque, Video,* vol. V ALGA Editores.
[155]*Guitar Review* N° 96; Interview by Gareth Walters 1994.

Classical guitarists become obsessed by the tone quality they produce with the fingers of their right hand. We spend almost as much time learning how to file and prepare our fingernails to get the best sound as we do practicing how to actually pluck the string. You can identify a classical guitarist by their phobia of losing a fingernail, and most guitarists learn not to use their right hands to fetch unseen objects out of drawers for example, in the hope of not spoiling a nail. Cardoor handles, zippers and flip-top lids are our natural enemies. Without right-hand fingernails, classical and flamenco guitarists are crippled as players, or in the words of Paco de Lucía, *"Like dancers without shoes."*[156]

Many flamenco guitarists criticise the classical guitarist's obsession for a fine warm tone because this sometimes means they'll sacrifice rhythmic precision just to get a good sound. And they're right. Paco de Lucía has made these objections, but some of his criticism comes from the fact that he's had to suffer the condescending manner with which many classical players have historically treated flamencos. The world famous classical guitarist Andrés Segovia criticised Paco de Lucía: *"That gentleman, Paco de Lucía, people think that just because he's got the facility to do some of those simple things he does, that he's a genius...any one of the young fellows coming up in the guitar competitions I attend has a fabulous technique, but all that 'pluck, pluck, pluck', that's not technique."*[157]

Paco de Lucía has never forgotten the way he was rejected by such established figures in the guitar world. About his recording of Joaquin Rodrigo's famous concierto de Aranjuez, Paco de Lucía said that he saw his opportunity to contribute something in his interpretation because he had never heard a classical guitarist perform it with the correct rhythm: *"The classical guitarist respects the sound and sometimes they abandon the rhythm in order to get the sound. If they move from one position to another, so as not to miss the note and make sure it's a good sound when they play it, they delay and pull a face as though they were doing it on purpose for artistic reasons. I prefer to hear an imperfect note than lose the rhythmic flow."*[158]

Backstage in London's Royal Festival Hall after a concert, I nervously told Paco de Lucía how much I liked his recording of the Concierto. Having checked my hands to see whether I was telling the truth about being a guitarist, he looked at me and said: "Well, Narciso Yepes didn't think much of it." Narciso Yepes (1927-1987), perhaps Spain's best known guitarist after Andrés Segovia, had been the first to record the Concierto and for many classical musicians his interpretation was unsurpassed.

"What does he know, anyway?" I jokingly replied.

"He's a *mamón*." Paco said, under his breath.

IS FLAMENCO GUITAR MUSIC WRITTEN DOWN?

Just like the songs and dances in flamenco, the music guitarists play is not traditionally written down. You learn the flamenco guitar by listening, watching and imitating. Flamenco guitar uses a very simple and logical jargon to describe hand positions and techniques. *Por medio*- in the middle- for example, is how they designate the chord shape of A major because the left hand looks like it's in the middle of the fret board. *Por arriba* - up high- is the term for the hand pattern made by the E minor chord which places most of the hand towards the bass side of the neck, which looks higher up, since the hand is moving towards the ceiling although this is where the lowest sounding notes are! In the classical guitar world the names of things are related to the rest of the classical music instrument family. The first string has the highest sound and so it's

---

[156]*El Mundo Magazine*, 1991
[157]*La Caña* magazine, N°. 28-29
[158]*Video Light & Shade*

called the top string, although it is physically closer to the ground. The sixth string has the lowest sound and so it's the bottom string. Flamenco players sometimes refer to the physical position of the string, calling the first string the bottom string, and the 6th string the top. Pressing the strings against the fretboard while moving the left hand along towards the body of the guitar raises the pitch of the notes, and so the positions of those frets are called the higher positions. Flamenco guitarists refer to them as 'down here' because that's where they are physically. The word *rasgeuo* comes from the word *rascar*- "to scratch." Not a particularly musical sounding technique but nevertheless descriptive of the action!

All written music is merely a *representation* of sound, it's not exact. Just as your passport photograph is not really you. The improvised feel of flamenco, like jazz, makes it hard to represent precisely in black and white. The music for the guitar was the first flamenco music to be written on the musical stave and there's no agreement yet over how to write the polyrhythms[159] of a seguiriyas or a bulerías. The rigidity of a written rhythm means that if you read the guitar music from the standpoint of a classically trained musician, you won't get the right feel. For example, although a piece may be written in 3/4 time, unless you feel the 6/8 count within that, you won't get the right flamenco feel. Vocally the music is so full of melismas and illogical stops and starts that it's practically impossible to write down. In any case, each representation of a flamenco form is a personal elaboration of a basic pattern which is unchanging. As soon as you write down music or a poem, it is fixed immovably in time and space. Classical musicians spend a lot of time and effort making sure they reproduce exactly what they see written on the page; contrary to what many flamencos think, this leaves ample room for personal interpretation. Just like a flamenco player reproducing a soleá or seguiriyas, each artist brings their own personality and character to the work.

MACHO MUSIC

Many aficionados will argue that the flamenco guitar has an inherently masculine sound which makes it impossible for a female to play. But that's as ridiculous as saying a female pianist can't play Prokofiev or Schostakovich because of the nature or tone of their works. If the performer is hidden from view, no one can tell whether the sound is being made by a man or a woman. My own belief is that the inherent differences between male and female physiognomy make it harder for women to build the stamina necessary for hours of *juerga*. Our muscles are simply not as developed as a man's and no matter how hard we try, they will not grow as strong as a man's. Although the flamenco guitar is physically easier to play than a standard classical instrument, the technique used involves more repetitive movements and therefore requires a stronger basic physiognomy.

WHY DON'T WOMEN PLAY THE FLAMENCO GUITAR?

During his travels through Spain in 1774 Sir Hugh Whiteford Dalrymple wrote a letter dated the 7th of July, in which he said, "*In the evening, some youngsters from the village got together at the doorstep of a small house where the barber who serves at the venta (inn, grocery store) lives. Among them was a young girl who played the guitar very pleasantly and sang seguidillas, a style of copla which they sing very animatedly.*"[160] This letter proves two things– that female guitarists are nothing new, and that the *seguidillas* is not the same as the *seguiriyas* we hear today.

---

[159]Polyrhythm is the amalgam of different rhythms
[160]*Historia del Flamenco, Vol. 1.*

In the past, many female flamenco performers accompanied themselves on guitar. José Blas Vega reports of the cantaor El Mochuelo (1868- 1937) singing for the celebrated dancer La Macarrona, who was accompanied on the guitar by a woman, Adela Cubas. They formed an artistic duo which continued to perform throughout the early 1900s.[161] However, as many of today's right-hand techniques require a lot of strength and stamina, it seems no female flamenco guitarist has yet been able to emulate her male contempories. Besides this, the flamenco guitar world is a male dominated field in the predominantly conservative and sexist society of rural Andalucia. Within Gypsy society it's still quite common for newly married women to be asked to abandon a performing career in favour of the traditional homemaker's role. Surely this is a branch of flamenco ripe for development, just as in the classical guitar world where women are gradually establishing themselves; it will take a few more generations of flamencos before the sight of a female flamenco guitarist becomes no more extraordinary than the sight of a female flamenco dancer in trousers.

---

[161]*El Mochuelo* CD, Sonifolk 20170.

CHAPTER 11: WHO WERE THE FAMOUS FLAMENCO GUITARISTS?

CANTE CON GUITARRA

Since Molina and Mairena's *Mundo y Formas* book, it has been accepted that the guitar was adapted to flamenco and gradually established the structure of the rhythms where previously songs were in free form. This opinion assumes that neither singers nor dancers had any basic sense of rhythm, which is hard to believe. The basis for all primitive musics is rhythm, a common denominator across cultures throughout the human race. Modern flamencologists such as José Manuel Gamboa and José Luís Ortiz Nuevo are successfully challenging some of the old dogma of flamenco, with the more logical assumption that the flamenco guitar evolved alongside flamenco song, since the guitar was already the most popular instrument throughout Spain during the late 18th Century and throughout the 1800s.

Of the long list of flamenco guitarists famous as accompanists and sometimes as soloists, a few from the mid 1800s are still regarded as innovators who influenced the direction the flamenco guitar has taken towards its position today, even though all we may have are written accounts of their styles. Just as with the history of famous cantaores, sometimes guitarists were well known for excelling in one particular style, or for their unique personality and *jondura* in their playing. Ingredients which meant certain figures became household names among aficionados, although nothing of their particular style has endured, as it was unique! Reading the descriptions of the playing styles and attributes of famous guitarists one eventually comes to the conclusion that each of them had the same outstanding gifts and abilities, but each developed in their own individualistic way: great picado, fantastic thumb dexterity, incredible falsetas, deep understanding of el cante, *flamencura, jondura, or gracia.* The differences are felt by individual listeners and each decides who is the greatest of them all according to their own criteria. A description of Ramón Montoya's contribution to the advancement of flamenco guitar technique is repeated in a description of the contributions of Niño Ricardo and Sabicas, but each of them took a step or two further into the unknowable future of the flamenco guitar.

Throughout the history of flamenco, certain guitarists have appeared who actually taught singers and dancers the basics of the forms. In this way the flamenco guitarist is often the guardian of flamenco, which shows how intimately related the instrument is to the development of the forms as we know them today. The dancer Vicente Escudero (1885-1980) holds a unique position as an innovator and creator, yet he was not originally a good Flamenco when it came to understanding the compás: *"No one would teach him the fundamentals of the dance, such as the compás, palmas etc."*[162] Eventually, Escudero turned to a guitarist to learn the irregular compás of the seguiriyas so that he could be the first to develop it into a dance.[163]

The flamenco guitar is just like the flamenco voice– individualistic; each guitarist's personality and sense of flamencura comes out in the sound of the strings as though they were vocal chords. For most aficionados the guitar is the flamenco instrument par excellence as it shadows, emulates and complements the voice superbly. Most of the developments in flamenco have come from the guitar, either in the hands of virtuoso players not content with the confines of accompanying singers or dancers, or in conjunction with experimental singers not content with the rigid confines of the song forms. Some of the evolution of forms can be heard today; Pepe Habichuela, for example, is largely responsible (along with Enrique Morente) for speeding up the seguiriya, drawing it closer to the bulerías rhythm as it shares the same basic 12 counts. Paco de Lucía has developed the tangos and tanguillos form into a more rhythmically complex palo than it used to be. The tanguillo was usually

---

[162]Don Pohren, *Lives and Legends of Flamenco*
[163]Paco Sevilla, Queen of the Gypsies

classed as a 'cante chico' because it was felt to be more frivolous than the tango and the dance is quite lascivious. In the hands of Paco de Lucía it has become one of flamenco's most demanding forms as it snakes between the internal 6/8 count alternating with 3/4 and 2/4.

Flamenco song and dance is nearly always accompanied by a guitar player who maintains the characteristic rhythmic cycle and the compás, but the guitar accompaniment was not always as elaborate as we're used to today. In the early days of flamenco, when the songs and dances which have evolved into what we recognize as flamenco were performed as part of the variety acts in café cantantes, the guitar was more of a tool of the trade than a musically valuable element. More than the limitations of the instrment, it was the limitations of the players which kept it confined to accompaniment, i.e., a few monotonoously strummed chords with few arpeggios, no picado and no tremolo. The guitar kept the compás for the dancers; the cante andaluz, which was eventually to be called cante flamenco, was secondary to the main attraction and many singers were their own accompanists. Without the capo or cejilla, accompaniment was limited to *por medio* and *por arriba*[164] which meant singers had to adapt their voices to the guitar's tonality, rather than the other way around. Fernando el de Triana (1867-1940) said this may have accounted for the gruffness of a cantaor's voice, since an almost toneless voice would not clash with the limited tones of the instrument.[165] Besides this, the effort of keeping the voice unnaturally low would lead to it losing its flexibility. The first flamenco guitar method published in 1902 by Rafael Marín hints at the poor technique of early flamenco guitarists: *"The tremolo is not used very much, and so to find a good player of the tremolo technique is difficult. The arpeggio isn't used much, he who knows of more than one is an exception. And chords are regularly used."*[166]

THE GUITAR'S EYEBROWS

It's thought the modern guitar didn't become a permanent accompanying instrument to flamenco singing before the invention of the *cejilla* or capo which raises the pitch, making the guitar a more versatile accompanying instrument. *Ceja* is the Spanish for 'eyebrow; *cejilla* means 'little eyebrow'! If you can raise the pitch of the basic key, then you can accompany many different voices: sopranos, tenors, contraltos, baritones and all the shades in between. In his autobiography, the famous classical guitarist Andrés Segovia recalled a travelling guitar player who gave him his first lessons: *"The guitarist produced his battered guitar, cracked here, its strings knotted over the rod which, tied to the neck, passed as a capo..."*[167]

With the adoption of the cejilla came a greater scope for guitarists and singers. Naturally the musicality of players began to develop beyond the artless strumming of two chords and the infinite possibilities of the instrument were slowly discovered. Although the cejilla was known in the 'classical' world of guitar playing, Anton Diabelli and Fernando Ferrandiere had both used it, the cejilla andaluza had not filtered down to the 'lower levels' of society until El Maestro Patiño (Cádiz 1829-1902) adopted it. Patiño probably came across this little device in the workshops of guitar makers who supplied both classical and flamenco players and those dedicated to *la guitarra del tablao*.[168]

---

[164]See, "Is Flamenco Guitar Music Written Down?"
[165]Silverio, Rey de Los Cantaores.
[166]*Ramón Montoya: El Genio de la Guitarra Flamenca* CD, Sonifolk 20130.
[167]Segovia, An Autobiography of the Years 1893-1920, Macmillan 1976.
[168]See Chapter 10, "La Guitarra de Tablao."

In his book *Paco de Lucía, Camarón de la Isla*[169] Felix Grande recounts an anecdote about El Camarón de La Isla and Caracol at the famous flamenco meeting point, the bar/hostel Venta Vargas in 1969, where the two cantaores alternated *tercios*. When Camarón was still a child, he had been taken to the Venta Vargas to sing for Caracol. The story goes that he was deeply hurt by Caracol's comment that his cante was no more than "not bad." On this occasion, Grande recounts how Camarón stood behind the aging Caracol, between him and the guitarist El Niño de Los Rizos (The Curly-Haired Kid):

"For a long time Camarón rested his hand on the back of Caracol's chair. Caracol was sitting down? He was sitting, but in each cante he rose up a bit, as though helping the cante to elevate. Other times he got hold of the table with his right hand, really grabbed it, as though asking the wood for strength. They had already sung por soleá, por seguiriya, por malagueña. Everything sounded like a seguiriya in those two voices. The fandangos also had the seguiriya's sounds of sorrow. I can see the scene. Caracol, flushed with the song, wine, and pain and bravura, sat in his wicker seat, inconsolably. On his left, el Niño de los Rizos playing por medio with the cejilla on the third fret. Between the two of them, Camarón de la Isla with his child-like face, resting his hand on the back of Caracol's chair. His younger voice going up and up like a mountain climber, precise and wise, the old man singing with his voice like a pot holer. Both of them in the same tone, both bewitched.

We sat half paralysed as though in a daguerreotype but with our pulses racing under our skins. We didn't know what was happening. You can't sing like that. But that's how they were singing in a 'worldly' way. Suddenly Camarón, with a tone of voice between casual, authoritative and affectionate, told Niño de los Rizos to raise the cejilla up a fret. Caracol didn't even look at him. He was "concentrated," to put it in the words García Lorca used to define el cante flamenco: "concentrated in himself and terrible in the midst of the shadow". So, they sang, with the cejilla on the fourth fret. It seemed as though the young fresh voice of Camarón was going to break the rough voice of Caracol in pieces. His voice cracked, but it didn't break. With each crack you could smell freshly spilled blood.

Camarón, with pitiless indifference, once again told El Niño de los Rizos to put the cejilla on the fifth. Caracol didn't even look at him. We didn't know what was happening. There, on the fifth fret por medio, you can't sing and yet that's where they were singing, and in a breathtaking way. So they sang fandangos with the cejilla on the fifth fret, por medio. One of them with a fresh voice; the other, with his voice trembling. The song burned both of them in their mouths. Now I know Camarón wanted to drag Caracol across the floor, but what was happening was that Caracol's fandangos, more and more mistreated, dragged in such a way that, rather than asking for pity, they distributed it– broken in pieces. Manolo Caracol gave with the generousness of the beggar. Camarón wanted to destroy him, he had destroyed him, but the more destroyed he was, Manolo Caracol was even more of a cantaor and maestro.

Camarón made a sign to el Niño de Los Rizos- no longer disdainful but a little inhibited- to make him raise the cejilla to the sixth fret. The noise of the cejilla against the strings echoed in the silence. Caracol didn't even look at him. Perhaps only the two of them knew what was going on. (...) It was merciless. It was also marvellous. Camarón de la Isla was bringing Caracol to his knees, but what was happening was that Caracol, with his voice on its knees, was all the more a maestro. They sang fandangos, taking turns, with the cejilla on the sixth." The 'fight' went on, until Camarón asked El Niño to put the cejilla on the 7th fret. Grande tells his story with inimitable poetry and describes the final reconciliation between the two *monstruos del cante*:

"Camarón felt reconciled at last. The proof is that when he sang a fandango with the cejilla on the 7th fret, instead of keeping his hand on the back of the chair, he rested it on the shoulder of Caracol. Like this, with

[169]Lunwerg editores 1998

his hand on the shoulder of his maestro, he sang with an anger which dissolved into pure exhaustion. When it was over, Caracol, without looking at him, -he looked at the floor, he looked beneath the floor - gave him a couple of affectionate pats on the hand."

Camarón was trying to publicly humiliate his 67-year-old idol, and prove to him that he was worthy of the older man's respect as a cantaor, since he could already sing him off the scale and off the stage. But as Caracol's voice became more and more ragged, his demeanour was more and more dignified, he would not give in to the younger singer's technical superiority. Caracol was subtly showing the younger man that it takes more than just technique and ability to be a true *cantaor*, it takes dignity, wisdom, and desperation.

The flamencologist José Blas Vega believes the capo was invented by the *gaditano* guitarist Patiño. Paco de Lucía recorded an *alegrías* in 1967 which he called "Recuerdo a Patiño"[170], in honour of this *tocaor* about whom the player Mario Escudero declared, *"You can't play a soleá without the four or five notes Patiño made it with."* Patiño has become famous as the first flamenco soloist, although he himself stated the guitar's purpose was to accompany the cante. He was a much soughtafter accompanist in his day, working alongside Siverio Franconetti, and later with don Antonio Chacón who declared him to be *"the most classic, the purest, the closest to the truth."*[171]

Among Patiño's disciples was Paco de Lucena, (1859-1898) born in Lucena in the province of Cordoba, hence his nickname, who worked in numerous café cantantes. De Lucena is credited with developing the musical structure of the *caña*, a song which many believe was the precursor to the *soleá*, and is mentioned in some of the earliest chronicles about flamenco. Today the caña is rarely sung, and it is Chacón's melodic version which predominates, opening with a series of 'ayes' with a liturgical air and based on the soleá compás. Among the disciples of Paco de Lucena was el Niño de Morón, born in Morón de la Frontera who is assumed to be the founder of the Morón School of guitarists whose most famous representative was Diego del Gastor.

FLAMENCO GUITAR SCHOOLS?
The Morón School

The Morón School, or style of playing is perhaps the most highly regarded to this day among connoisseurs of flamenco. Diego del Gastor (1908-1973), a Gypsy born in Ronda but who settled in the small town of Morón de la Frontera, between the provinces of Seville and Jerez came to symbolize all that was desirable and jondo in flamenco during the 1950s and '60s. To this day he is revered by all who get to know his playing through his meager recorded legacy. Foreign students of flamenco used to flock to Morón to learn from Diego, who was a reluctant teacher simply because he was not a man of routine. All around the world there are aficionados for whom Diego embodied flamenco almost as a guru embodies the beliefs of a religius sect. Today, one of the best ways to witness this legendary guitarist is on the series of videos Rito y Geografía del Toque (Ritual and Geography of Flamenco Guitar).[172] Here you can see Diego del Gastor perform with deceptively limited technical resources, (basically *horquilla*, *rasgeuo* and *pulgar*, i.e plucking bass and treble string simultaneously, rhythmic strumming, and playing melodies and *falsetas* predominantly with the thumb) but with more flamencura and *jondura* in one finger than most of the guitarists filmed in this series had in both hands. Sometimes a note doesn't come out, and sometimes an extra one does, slightly straying from *compás*, thus giving the lie to the rule that in order to play flamenco one must always be in *compás*. With a musical personality such as this, what would be

---

[170]*La Fabulosa Guitarra de Paco de Lucía,* Philips Polygram Iberica CD.
[171]*Silverio, Rey de Los Cantaores.*
[172]ALGA Editores, Spain.

considered a grave error in others becomes an added charm.

With his characteristic half smile, Diego phrases while looking around him, as though he were talking to his audience. His technique appears completely natural and instinctive, but for those who realise how hard it is to reach that level of simplicity, Diego del Gastor is an icon. The footage of him accompanying the *cantaor* Joselero de Morón in a *bulerías–alboreá* is simply a master class. On this video you can also see the famous footage from his live performance at the Moron Festival of Bulerías, the origin of the '*graciosa*' (charming, witty, funny) falseta which turns up twenty years later, with a peculiarly contemporary feel, performed by Raimundo Amador of Pata Negra.[173]

Diego's two nephews Paco (b. 1944 Francisco Gómez Amaya) and Dieguito de Morón (b.1947 Diego Torres Amaya) continue his legacy although the latter is perhaps more like his uncle in that he can rarely be found performing in concert. Diego has very firm convictions about the flamenco guitar today:

"Today of all the current guitarists, I don't like a single one of them because they don't move me; there's no artistic personality. I know how they all play, I know what they give of themselves and apart from Morón, I don't like anybody. Do you know what it is like to destroy someone artistically? Well, Paco de Lucía can destroy every one of them, he can cut them up into pieces. The only one he can't handle is me, I'd like him to understand, only he knows this already. Paco doesn't blow me apart. Apart from the monster of my uncle Diego, the one I most like in the world is me and after that, Paco de Lucía."[174]

Paco del Gastor is known today as the accompanist to Fernanda de Utrera, and more recently of El Cabrero, a popular cantaor who specialises in fandangos with socially relevant lyrics. He also plays with the jondura typical of Morón but has a more virtuosic technique and loves the style of Paco de Lucía with whom he toured in the 1970s and formed a lasting friendship. On the Morón School, Gastor has commented, *"Of course all of the modern players have learned from the toque of Morón- if not, how would they know how to play por bulerías? What happened is that Paco adapted it to his abilities. Besides, nobody can play the pure way that Diego played."*[175]

The Jerez School

The Moraos of Jerez, along with Parilla de Jerez (Manuel Fernández Molina b.1945) represent another individual style of playing– a thumb driven, rhythmically intense style best illustrated by the Jerez style of bulerías. This line of playing is traced back to Javier Molina (1868-1956), a famous accompanist in his day who taught Manuel Morao (b.1929)[176], founder of the present day company known as Gitanos de Jerez which is dedicated to the promotion and continuation of a Gypsy style of flamenco in all its aspects. In his early days Manuel was known as Moraíto de Jerez and his younger brother Juan (1935-2002), also a guitarist, went under the name Moraíto Chico. Now, Juan's son goes by this same artistic name. Moraito Chico (b. 1956) continues along the stylistic lines of his father and uncle, combining the fresh feel of modern flamenco with a jondura few others possess. He accompanies José Mercé, the Gypsy cantaor from Jerez also known for his jondura. Moraito Chico's son, Diego de Morao (b.1979) presently continues in his father's and grandfather's footsteps with, miraculously, the same flamencura so highly prized by aficionados.

---

[173]See Chapter 13, "What is Flamenco Fusion?"
[174]CD *Dieguito de Morón,* Cultura Jonda 21 Fonomusic.
[175]*A New Tradition for the Flamenco Guitar*, Paco Sevilla, Sevilla Press 1995.
[176]See Chapter 7, "Are All Flamencos Gypsies?"

Guitarists have often been instrumental (pardon the pun) in the continuation of certain styles, such as Perico el del Lunar[177](1894-1946) who was another of Javier Molina's students and therefore considered a member of the Jerez school. Perico compiled the famous *Antología del Cante Flamenco,* the first of its kind, originally produced in France in 1954. Perico sometimes actually taught the cantes to the cantaores involved in this recording. The sleeve notes to this landmark recording were written by the musicologist Tomás Andrade de Silva, who was professor of chamber music at the Madrid conservatory. Hardly an expert on flamenco or even folk music, de Silva relied heavily on Perico for the information as he was acknowledged as the: *"mature guardian of the secrets of his art and possessor of a privileged memory, the only individual who could bestow upon the anthology the joint honour of artistry and requisite musicology."*

Tomás Andrade de Silva acknowledged Perico's authority thus:

"The guitarist Perico el del Lunar was one of the outstanding figures of the art of flamenco, through him even forgotten styles had their resurrection. There was not a single cante nor guitar falseta he didn't know, and if he knew the structure of the creations by the 'old masters' from Breva and Silverio to Chacón and la Trini, he knew even better the miraculous improvisations of the guitarists Paco de Lucena and Patiño." Perico had the good fortune to be born in an age when some historically important flamencos were still active, accompanying Chacón and working alongside Ramón Montoya.

The Granada School

Juan Carmona Carmona, Juan Habichuela (b.1933) holds a privileged position today as the patriarch of a dynasty of flamencos which includes two of the founding members of the pop-flamenco band Ketama. He is not known as a soloist, but quite simply as the best accompanist alive today. To speak of a Granada school is something of an exaggeration, unlike Jerez or Morón there are no specific traits which distinguish players such as Juan or his brother Pepe (b. 1944 José Antonio Carmona Carmona) or other players from Granada such as Paco Cortes (b. 1957) except perhaps in their uniquely 'oriental' feel for the *tangos.*

THE EMPEROR OF THE GUITAR

One of the most influential artistic personalities in the flamenco guitar was Ramón Montoya (1879- 1949) a Gypsy who also learned from Paco de Lucena, incorporating techniques developed by classical players such as Emilio Pujol and Miguel Llobet. Montoya became Chacón's accompanist, learning to differentiate between his solo playing and his role as accompanist, limiting the picado which dazzled in his solos to a musically intelligent aspect of accompaniment. At this time, when the techniques of players were blossoming, cantaores would sometimes find themselves in a battle for attention as guitarists couldn't resist the temptation to display their skills.

Montoya completed the structure of the solo for guitar known as the Rondeña which is unique in flamenco for using the tuning which is typical of a lute: the third string is tuned to F$\sharp$ and the sixth string to D. The Rondeña was first developed by Miguel Borrull (1866-1926) who studied with the famous classical guitarist Francisco Tárrega. Tárrega was in turn a student of Julian Arcas (1832-1882), the first guitarist to include flamenco works in his concert repertoire. Perhaps the knowledge Borrull gained from Tárrega about the classic rules of harmony allowed him the freedom to experiment with archaic tunings and come up with something so innovative. When Montoya became the most important guitarist in Spain and was holding court at the Villa Rosa flamenco venue in the center of Madrid, he used to tease other guitarists by handing them his guitar after playing a

---

[177]The nickname means "Perico, He of the Mole" which refers to a mole he eventually had removed from his face.

Rondeña with this tuning, so that they could have the opportunity to show their worth before the great master. Ignorant of the secret of the altered tunings, the players would attack the guitar with gusto only to find they produced an ugly mess of sounds.[178]

There is no doubt that even today's players owe a debt to Montoya for his contribution to the flamenco guitar's musical development, and most contemporary players will mention his name when asked about their influences. Either directly from his recordings, or indirectly through the number of followers of his style, Montoya's legacy is still alive today.

A TIME OF TITANS

With Montoya came a generation of guitarists who have all left their mark on the art, most of whom also worked in the Villa Rosa. Manolo de Huelva (1892-1976) was another follower of Paco de Lucena and became the official accompanist for contestants during the 1922 Concurso de Cante Jondo in Granada. Manolo was never interested in recording and despite the fact that he accompanied artists with extensive discographies such as La Niña de Los Peines and Manuel Torres, the only testimony we have of his unique and influential playing is word of mouth. Sabicas (Agustín Castellón Campos 1907-1990) learned from Manolo, and declared Manolo's playing to be more 'gitano' than the Gypsy Montoya, who barely ever had a good word to say about any other guitarist except Manolo de Huelva. The world famous classical guitarist Andrés Segovia recalled Manolo as "the best when I was young"[179].

In the list of flamenco guitar legends, after Montoya comes Sabicas who made his debut at the age of ten and joined the lineup of guitarists at the Villa Rosa at the age of thirteen. Sabicas developed his solo playing beyond the legacy of Montoya, exploiting the whole range of the instrument's capabilities rather than using just a few classical techniques. His picado and arpeggio extended into the bass strings, he used the alzapúa technique across all six strings rather than confining himself to just the basses, and he used several guitaristic tricks which always astound non-guitarists but are actually not technically difficult at all. These included using the left hand to cross two bass strings over one another so that they rattle together when plucked, producing a sound exactly like a snare drum, or playing complete melodic passages with just the left hand pulling and "hammering" on the strings over the fretboard. Both of these techniques had been used in classical guitar compositions well before Sabicas stunned his audiences with them[180], and neither technique has a uniquely flamenco aspect about it. Sabicas played with what could be called a 'classic flamenquismo', the clean technique and clarity of notes which were normal aspects in classical playing; these qualities became requirements in flamenco as well largely because of Montoya and Sabicas. Every note could be heard, and every note had a purpose. Increasingly, flamenco guitarists were expected to be perfect accompanists and perfect soloists. For many guitar aficionados it is precisely the crisp accuracy of Sabicas and Montoya, Pepe Martínez (1923-1984) Serranito (b.1942) and others from this 'school' which makes their playing less flamenco than slightly less technically virtuoso performers such as the Morón dynasty, or the hundreds of less well known accompanists whose names may never be recorded for posterity.

CLASSIC FLAMENCO COMPOSERS?

Luís Maravilla (b.1914 Luis López Tejera) was another youngster who eventually went to work at the

---

[178]Perico El del Lunar, Un Flamenco de Antología.
[179]*Diccionario Enciclopédico de Flamenco.*
[180]Napoleon Coste 1806-1883.

Villa Rosa. The son of cantaor El Niño de las Marianas, Luís went under his family name until a competition in 1928 in which the dictator Primo de Rivera was a jurist. Hearing the young Luisito, Rivera who was a serious aficionado declared, "My vote is for that young boy who is a *maravilla* on the guitar."[181] *Maravilla* means "marvel" in Spanish. Fascinated by the classical guitar after witnessing a concert by Andrés Segovia, he took lessons from Miguel Llobet in Barcelona. With his solid grounding in solfa, Maravilla was able to write down his own works and published one of the first flamenco guitar methods. He was also the first flamenco guitarist to perform the most famous work for classical guitar and orchestra by Joaquin Rodrigo, the *Concerto de Aranjuez* in 1952.

When it comes to actual compositions for the flamenco guitar, Esteban Sanlúcar (b.1910) is the best known as his works have been recorded by Paco de Lucia; Sanlúcar works include *The Panaderos Flamencos* and *Mantilla de Feria* . El Niño Ricardo's works, or versions, were also published; although having been transcribed primarily by a pianist these versions were unplayable! Guitarists learn by repetition and experimentation to get the sound they have stuck in their ears to come out of the strings. El Niño Ricardo's versions have been performed so often by various soloists that they are 'standards' in most repertoires. For example a version of soleares and alegrías which are basically Niño Ricardo's creations appear regularly in the repertory of England's well known flamenco guitarist Paco Peña[182] (b. 1942). As Ricardo (1904-1972) had such a powerful influence on so many guitarists who are at the summit of their careers today, -Paco de Lucía has said: *"we all copied Niño Ricardo."*- so his reputation as a revolutionary creator survives. As Montoya lies further removed in history, so his influence, or the recognition of it, recedes. As with the historic cantaores, it is those who have made recordings who will survive in the collective memory and to whom we shall continue to refer to as pioneers.

Serranito (Victor Monge b. 1942) was one of the first to formally compose written works for the flamenco guitar and orchestra. He decided to focus on solo concert performing although his early career, like so many others, evolved through accompanying in some of Madrid's most famous tablaos. This is an aspect of utmost importance to a solo guitarist as any flamenco composition, in order to be flamenco, must contain the fundamentals of el cante and compás, elements which only an apprenticeship can provide. Serranito is best known for his concert performing and composing for films and official events such as the 1988 Universal Expo in Australia where his work represented Spain.

Manolo Sanlúcar (b.1943) is another guitarist whose artistic personality has led him into formal composition, crossing from the boundaries of traditional flamenco into the boundaries of classical music. Along with Paco de Lucía, Manolo Sanlúcar is considered one of the most important figures in flamenco of the past 50 years. These two maestros have quite different approaches to their playing, reflected in their different careers. Where Paco de Lucía has become perhaps the world's best known Spanish guitarist *per se*, Manolo Sanlúcar has become something of a prophet within Spain but is not as widely known abroad. Flamenco aficionados generally are divided into two camps–those who eulogise Paco and those who eulogise Manolo! There is, however, no rivalry at all between them; on the contrary, they are close friends who admire one another's work unconditionally. One of the highlights of Carlos Saura's *Sevillanas* movie is the charming duo these two *monstrous* (giants) of flamenco guitar perform together.

Besides his work as an accompanist to some of the best singers, Manolo Sanlúcar has composed works for the Ballet Nacional de España as well as works for guitar and orchestra, these include his *Fantasía* which premiered in 1978, and *Trebujena* (1987). *Tauromágia* (1987) has been called the best flamenco guitar recording ever, as it embodies not only Sanlúcar's uniquely rich musicality but also the essence of flamenco and

[181]*Luis Maravilla por Derecho,* M. Espín, J.M Gamboa, 1990.
[182]Paco Peña was born in Spain but his career has developed mainly in the United Kingdom. Unfortunately, in Spain he does not receive the recognition he deserves, particularly as the instigator and founder of the world famous Cordoba Guitar Festival.

flamenco guitar. Sanlúcar has always fought to bring the public's estimation of the flamenco guitar up to the same level as that of the classical guitar. By teaching the structure and rules which surround flamenco forms he has shown many classical academics that flamenco is not a folk art without foundations, but a complex art which can be discussed using the same terms as one would use in classical music. In the early 1970s he recorded a trilogy *Mundo y Formas de la Guitarra* which "contains the most complete catalogue of falsetas in all the styles."[183] His dedication and serious approach to teaching has produced a string of disciples who continue to enrich the flamenco guitar landscape, such as Rafael Riqueni (b.1962), Vicente Amigo (b.1967), and Juan Carlos Romero (b.1964) each of whom have developed a unique compositional language and approach to their playing.

The differences between the Gypsy performer and non-Gypsy in flamenco are the same whether they are guitarists or cantaores or bailaores. It is rare to find a Gypsy dedicated to teaching and the more intellectual ideal of improving flamenco's image among non-flamencos. Gypsy guitarists such as Diego del Gastor who studied solfa were extremely rare in his day, now it is common for flamenco guitarists Gypsy or otherwise to study in formal music institutions while continuing their traditional flamenco apprenticeship. The young Jerónimo Maya (b. 1977) is one of those rare Gypsy guitarists studying music in a formal institution, while accompanying masters of el cante such as Chano Lobato as well as developing a very exciting personal style. Since these institutions have also become more open minded and now teach things like jazz harmony just as readily as classical, it is less surprising to hear of flamencos who have done their three or four years of formal musical studies. Paco Peña became the first professor of flamenco in Rotterdam and already guitarists from his home town of Córdoba are travelling to Holland to follow the programme of studies there[184]!

THE SUMMIT

Ramón Montoya was the ultimate guitarist in his day. Then along came Sabicas, who became known as *the phenomenon*, but Sabicas basically continued along the same artistic lines. Now the guitarist Paco de Lucía has become the marker dividing a before and after in the history of flamenco[185]. Words fail us when trying to describe the technique, flamencura and musicianship of this guitarist from Algeciras (b. 1947). Many words have already been written about him and many more will be written. Paco de Lucía is an artist who transcends the label of flamenco. Listening to his latest CD *Luzia* one is aware how he has transcended technique, and without doubt Paco de Lucía has *the* most astounding technique of any flamenco guitarist and I would include most classical performers in a comparative list. Paco de Lucía forgot about technique in his teens, his virtuosity is unparalleled and for him, uninteresting.

It is his constant seeking out of new harmonies and different ways to say what flamenco has been saying for hundreds of years that caused a revolution in flamenco guitar and which has affected every other aspect of the art. Often referred to as a 'universal flamenco', Paco's music has a personal stamp and profound flamencura which extends into whatever collaboration he is involved with. Teaming up with jazz guitarists or performing the classical works of Manuel de Falla or Joaquin Rodrigo, his sound is quite simply *flamenco*. Besides this important quality, Paco is a *musician*. With no formal training at all, still unable to read sheet music, Paco de Lucía's flamenco compositions contain ingredients few non-classically trained guitarists dominate: sense of structure, development and harmonic progression, intelligent distribution of voicing, melody and ornament, and something even harder to learn: good taste.

Commentators have discerned three stages in Paco de Lucía's development so far, each of which has

[183]J.M Gamboa, *Guía Libre del Flamenco,* SGAE 2001.
[184]Paco Serrano, b. 1964.
[185]See Chapter 15, "What is Flamenco Nuevo?"

had a profound and lasting effect on flamenco. His initial stage as a soloist can be followed through his discography which stands as testimony to his personal evolution, developing a unique language. Following his meeting with Camarón de La Isla he revolutionised flamenco guitar accompaniment. With the formation of his sextet including percussion, bass guitar, flute and saxophone as well as the traditional elements of cante and baile, he founded the now standard flamenco lineup. Every solo flamenco performer since Paco de Lucía now performs with a similar group, from Enrique del Melchor in the 1970s through to Vicente Amigo in the present day. His collaborations with jazz musicians opened up another seam which is still being mined by such players as J. Manuel Cañizares and Gerardo Nuñez. Even Jerónimo Maya born in 1977, five years before the release of *Passion, Grace and Fire,*[186] performs Paco/Di Meola/McLaughlin-style duos with his brother Felipe in concert today.

In the history of flamenco, most agree that Paco de Lucía quite simply represents the art worldwide, and is, without a doubt, the most important figure ever to have emerged in the flamenco guitar. Listening to a selection of his discography is far more revealing, and satisfying than reading the vast amounts which have been published about his person and his art.

---

[186]Phillips 811 344-2

CHAPTER 12: WHAT IS DUENDE?

"Duende" is a little spirit, what the Irish call a leprechaun; a mischievous elf. In 1933, during a lecture/recital tour of Argentina, Federico García Lorca (1898-1936) told an incredulous journalist that his 'duende'- his inspirational spirit had taken on corporeal form and visited him at the foot of his bed:

"It was already two in the morning, but Belladonna hadn't closed my eyelids. Sleep wouldn't come. I turned out the light. Almost immediately, at the foot of my bed I made out a figure ..., a kind of strange, surprisingly agile doll who started to jump up and down on the bed frame. It measured about 30 centimetres tall. Dressed in red and yellow, he wore slippers with a pointed toe and on his head a green cap with a tiny bell on its tip.... I swear to you, I was as awake as I am now ...the duende (what else could it have been?) climbed with a fantastic jump onto the wardrobe. I heard the thump, the solid impact of his feet as they struck the wood. From there, with his arms bent at his sides, very stiff and lively he fixed me with his tiny pupils with purple reflections while, with comic seriousness, he moved his face from left to right and the little bell on his cap rang."[187]

This light-hearted, teasing vision of a mischievous spirit is very different from the serious, mysterious and elusive inspirational spirit called 'duende flamenco', probably also invented by García Lorca.

In his famous conference on the *Historic and Artistic Importance of the Primitive Canto Andaluz Called Cante Jondo* given in 1922 on the eve of the competition in Granada, Lorca doesn't mention 'duende', neither in the joking context nor the inspirational context. It is only in the 1930s, having revised the speech for a tour in South America, that he began to use it. In Demófilo's collection of Cantes Flamencos published in 1881 there is no mention of *duende flamenco*, and so it would appear to be García Lorca's contribution to the vocabulary of flamenco. The poet was always fascinated by the Gypsys' ability to lose themselves in their cante, this was what he eventually called *duende*, a term which still causes arguments and exasperation within flamenco. García Lorca is said to have heard the singer Diego el Lebrijano (1847- ?) say, *"On the days when I sing with duende, nobody can equal me."*

Manuel Torres (1878-1933), a contemporary of García Lorca and Manuel de Falla is said to have commented, "Everything that has dark sounds has duende,"[188] after hearing extracts of Falla's composition *Noches en los Jardines de España*, written in 1915. In the original Spanish he says *sonidos negros*- "black sounds"- which may have been a reference to the black keys on the piano, or the sharps and flats typical of the minor intervals in flamenco. From this period onwards, the term entered flamenco's vocabulary to the acceptance of some and rejection of others. Antonio Mairena used it to describe the indescribable condition of being Gypsy[189], and each cantaor has his or her own idea of what this word represents, generally boiling down to a 'state of grace' or inspiration which no one can predict. My experience and understanding of duende, both in live performance of flamenco and personal experience while performing, is that it is a moment when art is produced unconsciously, a moment when the unconscious or intuitive aspect of a performance dominates over the technically polished. When the mind and thinking and controlling technique take a back seat. It is not something limited to flamenco performers, but can be witnessed during classical and jazz concerts, and can be found in sculpture and paintings by such genius as Rodin or Michelangelo.

The difficulty all cantaores have in describing or explaining el duende doesn't mean they don't agree it can exist, but there's no unique definition of it, no agreement over what it is.

---

[187]F. García Lorca, *Prosa*. 1 Akal S.A, 1994.
[188]"Manuel de Falla y El Cante Jondo" E.Molina Fajardo Ed. Universidad de Granada, 1962.
[189]See "What's the Gypsy's Story?" Disembodied Reason.

El Camarón de la Isla put it like this:

"I think you can find duende in most jobs, but probably more in ours, in the Gypsy's. But you can't explain it. The duende is that inspiration that you don't know when is going to arrive. It makes you do something you've never done before. Everybody can have it, but it's more of a Gypsy thing. But it's not possible to explain it. Me, sometimes I'll do something in el cante that I've never done before and I'll never do again because I wouldn't know how to repeat it. Maybe that's it."[190]

And for José Mercé it is like this:

It's very hard to explain. I'd say this: sometimes when you perform or record or meet friends, you think, "I'd give anything not to sing today, because you just don't feel like it." But as a professional you have to give everything, so that day somehow you go out on stage and it turns out to be better than ever- I think that must be el duende.[191]

When a performer transmits this unique state, it can drive audiences wild; sometimes the performer will be unaware that he or she is actually performing with duende. El Chocolate put it like this: *"Sometimes the audience really likes what I do. I don't like it, but the public loves it. That must be because you can't really listen to yourself. It's very difficult to understand, a mystery. You don't like yourself and the audience really loves it, That's* el duende."[192]

The writer and poet Fernando Quiñones recalled a vivid moment in performance when the effects of duende overpowered Caracol: *"Caracol sang por bulerías, and then Chano Lobato sang; afterwards they took turns. The cante grew in tension, in quality, and despite his lack of agility, Caracol gave a jump and moved his solid body in a little baile thus confirming with this improvised moment, lightly touched with humour, John Dos Passos' beautiful observation on the occasional comic interlude in the art of flamenco which after some emotionally dense moments take the role of 'the baby sitter who tries to distract the child after having told him something too terrible.'*

But the bulerías intensified. Caracol and Lobato took that cante to unknown aesthetic and emotional heights. Transported, one of the Gypsies present bit hard on the shoulder of his friend, but he didn't have to excuse himself since this fellow, also totally absorbed, didn't even notice. Soon there is laughter, there are tears; cries ring out on the patio. Quickly, humour and pain get mixed up and blend in the cante; there's no way to distinguish them, and the baroque, growing rhythm of the palmas, feet and voices is more intoxicating than the cheapest wine from Chiclana passed around. With Chano Lobato's last few verses of bulerías, Caracol loses his mind. Crying as if he were suffocating, he brings his hand up to his shirt collar and begins tearing at it determinedly, down to his waist to offer it in homage to the other cantaor."[193]

Tearing one's shirt or clothing in response to extreme emotion is a traditionally Gypsy act. At Camarón's funeral several Gypsies did just that, tore their shirts in shreds in an exaggerated and dramatic gesture of grief. Women tear their hair; men tear their shirts.

[190]Interview, *El Europeo.*
[191]José Mercé, interview by Emma Daly, *Newsweek*, February 12, 2001.
[192]El Chocolate interviewed by M. Mora, *El País*, October 25th, 2001.
[193]A. A. Caballero, *El Cante Flamenco* p. 205-6.

Moments such as this, although rare, are not always referred to as *duende*. Expressions such as *aire* or *angel* (an air or angel) are more often used in Andalucía and by Flamencos themselves. The term *duende* has been abused and romanticised and, perhaps because it came from outside the flamenco community in the first place, flamencos themselves will rarely use it. Yet they don't want to reject it since the exclusivity tag is highly valued in flamenco, and duende is a phenomenon which has been linked exclusively to flamenco. *Duende* is a term most often used by critics and commentators to describe flamenco, it has its roots in the intelligentsia or intellectual aficionados who are traditionally disdained by the flamenco community.

CHAPTER 13: WHAT IS FLAMENCO FUSION?

"Flamenco fusion" is yet another label, an umbrella term under which most experiments get grouped. There are countless examples of so-called flamenco-rock, flamenco-pop, or jazz-flamenco, and in practically every case, what you get is not a fusion but collaboration. *Fusion* means you fuse -join together- different elements and end up with something new and original, a style with its own unique properties easily distinguished from another. When musicians from two different disciplines get together, without rehearsal or stylistic guidelines what generally happens is each group of artists will simply do what they do, no matter what instrument you give them. The earliest flamenco 'fusion' on record was Ramón Montoya accompanying the saxophone player Fernando Vilches[194], where the saxophone simply took the role of a cantaor. Neither instrumentalist was straying outside the patterns of flamenco. Flamenco is itself a fusion of cultural and musical styles, which has resulted in the set of palos- patterns- we recognise as flamenco. It contains ingredients from Arabic, Sefardic and Asian music which, combined with a unique Andalusian and Gypsy interpretation, gives us what we have today. Those who try to 'unravel' the mysteries of flamenco's past are not really doing it any favors. It is a unique musical style with its own identity and values, just like Arabic, Sefardic or Asian music today.

The similarities with Asian music has led to collaborations, 'fusions' and creations attempting to prove a common source. When Gualberto[195] accompanied a singer on the sitar, he played the it in the same way he would play the guitar, using the same phrasing and the same compás. It was nothing new, just flamenco played on a sitar. If the sitar were played in an Indian raga, perhaps in a flamenco compás and combined with a cantaor singing a strict flamenco form, then you might have something new. The collaboration of Pepe Habichuela with the Bollywood strings[196] has produced some attractive sounds, but not a fusion of styles. Rather, we have a flamenco guitarist performing alongside an Indian violinist and sitar player using conventional flamenco compás. Perhaps the most striking of these Asian-flamenco get togethers was the brief collaboration of flamencos with the Karnataka College of Percussion who gave a highly successful series of concerts uniting the Kathak northern Indian dance style with flamenco compás. Their performances confirmed a common origin and the musicians experienced a sense of familiarity with one another's styles, but it did not result in a new musical form, rather it served to highlight how individual cultures with the same basic ingredients will eventually evolve a different musicality.

FUSION OR CONFUSION?

Many aficionados who came to flamenco during the 1950s and 60s can't get used to the idea of flamenco mixing with instruments from outside the traditional flamenco boundaries. Paco de Lucía's inclusion of sax and flute, bass guitar, 'ud and percussion horrified almost as many people as it delighted. Those who agreed with Mairena's assertions about purity wanted to find a different label for such mixtures, since what they heard didn't sound like flamenco to them. When Paco de Lucía started introducing unusual chords into his playing, he was fusing a new element with flamenco. In the late '70s he teamed up with jazz guitarists Al di Meola, John McLaughlin and Larry Coryell, and learned how to improvise; forever changing the flamenco guitar.

---

[194]Ramón Montoya: El Genio de la Guitarra Flamenca, Grabaciónes Históricas 1923-1936, Sonifolk CD 20130.
[195]Gualberto García Pérez, founding member of Andalucian rock band Smash, See "Flamenco's Generation X" in Chapter 15.
[196]Pepe Habichuela & The Bollywood Strings, *Yerbagüena*, Nuevos Medios 15 788 CD.

But he recognised that:

"fusion can have good results, although I don't believe in it. In my work with these guitarists the music wasn't jazz nor flamenco, it was more a fusion of musicians than of musical styles."[197] There is no question that what Paco de Lucía played was flamenco; in compás, and emotional context, but he was developing a language which has since become the standard for practically every flamenco guitarist since, whether in accompaniment or as soloist.

In every instance of fusion of cantaor with unusual harmonies on the guitar, the sitar or violin, it is the cante which remains flamenco, that carries the flamencura, and identifies the form. If the cante is changed, then it will either not be flamenco any more, or it will be an evolution of a form or be something entirely new.

JAZZ FLAMENCO- FLAMENCO JAZZ

Flamenco guitar players have had no difficulty incorporating jazz chord inversions and harmonies into flamenco. Juan Manuel Cañizares and Gerardo Nuñez both cross the boundaries between the two traditions, often producing astonishing results such as Cañizares' accompaniment of Enrique Morente's Seguiriya on Carlos Saura's movie *Flamenco* in which he adjusts the tuning of the instrument to access deeper bass notes and a wider range of intervals.[198] Morente sings a traditional seguiriyas despite the difficulty in maintaining the melody when confronted by such unusual harmonies. Other masterful cantaores such as Carmen Linares and Estrella Morente show a depth of musicality which goes beyond the limits of flamenco traditions by maintaining the identity of the cantes even when their accompanists are using un-flamenco accompaniment. These kinds of collaborations, involving other instrumentalists, such as double bass or cello, flute, saxophone or Arabic 'ud are beginning to find their own identity within flamenco. They are so distinct from the traditional sounds of the guitar of Manuel Morao accompanying Terremoto, for example, that they seem to be impostors from a foreign land. Yet the basic identity is flamenco, maintaining the patterns and compás and emotional content, and thus it receives the title Flamenco Nuevo.[199]

Spanish jazz has its own identity, quite distinct from American jazz. Players such as Chano Dominguez and Jorge Pardo have absorbed a flamenco feeling which is inescapable in their playing. Pardo plays jazz with 'angel' and flamencura, often using the ornaments and melodic style of a cantaor, particularly in his flute playing. Chano Dominguez also uses flamenco compás and modes in his jazz piano, combined with a peculiarly *Spanish* sound which can trace its roots back to classical composers and performers Enrique Granados (1867-1916) and Manuel de Falla (1876-1946). Spanish musicians can't escape the heritage which feeds their subconscious and affects their interpretations. Who can resist the colour and intensity of Alicia de Larocha's interpretations of Albéniz or Falla compared to any other performer? Likewise, who can deny the flamencura of Paco de Lucía's performance of Rodrigo's *Concerto de Aranjuez*?

NUEVO ARABIGO- ANDALUZ?

Quite a few Flamencos feel a special affinity with Arabic music. The two cultures, Spanish and North African, share many similarities dating back to the days of Al-Andalus, which throughout Arabic speaking lands is normally referred to with a degree of inexplicable nostalgia. Inexplicable because it cannot remain in the collective memory so many centuries after its passing, yet some lingering after taste has been

---

[197] *Historia-Guia del Nuevo flamenco*, Ediciones Guia de Musica.
[198] See Chapter 1, "The Musical Nitty Gritty."
[199] See Chapter 15, "What Is Flamenco Nuevo?"

subconsciously nurtured: *"The Arabs and the Muslims have all silently and without conferring selected Al-Andalus as an ever abiding memory in their hearts."*[200] Despite the apparent separation of Spanish and Moorish cultures– most Spaniards hate to admit the similarities, long preferring to identify themselves with a kind of European standard culture (again due to some inexplicable after taste of the so-called *occupation* no body can possibly remember)–Tunisia and Morocco are number one Spanish tourist destinations. The immediate feeling of *hermandad* -brotherhood and recognition- sensed between Spaniards and North African cultures is an unspoken reality. Lole Montoya of the duo Lole Y Manuel who were popular during the 1970s nearly always sings something in Arabic, learned from her mother Antonia La Negra who was born in Oran and who grew up hearing both flamenco and Algerian music. Lole's ex-husband Manuel Molina grew up in Ceuta, the Spanish city perched on the edge of the Muslim world. Their affinity with Moorish culture is in their blood and reflected in their performances and recordings.

Another fine example of attempts to 'reunite' flamenco with Arabic roots came with Juan Peña "El Lebrijano" and his 1983 collaborations with the Orquesta Andalusí from Tangiers in a recording which sold 200,000 copies, a lot for such a non-commercial music as flamenco. For a few years aficionados thought they had lost El Lebrijano to this commercially successful adventure, as he withdrew from 'standard' flamenco to concentrate on just *Encuentro*[201]. His more recent CD *Casablanca*[202] was presented as a follow-on to this, a compelling collaboration with Moroccan musician Faical Kourrich of such intense musicality and artistry that the results reach beyond the boundaries of labels such as 'flamenco' or 'traditional'.

The poetry of El Lebrijano's words still contain the seed of Arabic poetry:

En tu boca roja fresca, beso mi sed	In the fresh scarlet of your lips, I kiss my thirst
y no se apaga	And am not quenched
Y en cada beso quisiera beber entera	And in each kiss, I wish to drink
tu alma	Your entire soul

The guitarist Vicente Amigo has also found an affinity with Arabic music. Each of his tangos has an indescribably middle eastern flavour, despite the fact that this palo originated as one of the Black African dances popular during the 16th Century!

FLAMENCO- ROCK

Enrique Morente has said he would have loved to be a rock singer. Both in live performance and on CD[203] he uses the rock band Lagartija Nick to 'fuse' rock with flamenco. The primitive force of rock music has a lot in common with flamenco, a directness and immediacy many flamencos can identify with. Raimundo Amador, along with his brother Rafael, formed the flamenco-rock band *Pata Negra*[204] in 1987 where they invented the *blueserías* , an infectious Gypsy-flamenco-blues played to bulerías compás, and sang lyrics which only made sense to those familiar with marginal neighbourhoods of Andalucian cities where petty crime and the Gypsy population were becoming synonymous. Pata Negra represent an indigenous flamenco-rock based on the instinctive talents of the guitar playing of Raimundo and his brother, sometimes incorporating the

[200]Salma Khadra Jayyusi, *The Legacy of Muslim Spain, Foreword.*
[201]Ariola, S.A.
[202]Hemisphere EMI.
[203]Omega CD, *El Europeo Musica* 001
[204]'Black Leg' is the name for the Spanish breed of pig from which the delicacy of cured ham is produced.

falsetas of a few legendary flamenco guitarists such as Diego del Gastor.[205] Raimundo was brought up in a flamenco atmosphere, accompanying members of his family and well known cantaors like Lole Y Manuel and Enrique Morente and his playing is fundamentally flamenco, even when improvising a blues on stage with B.B King. His playing crosses the borders between blues and flamenco with astounding facility and today he is considered the leader of the *flamenco-rock-gitano style*, of which he is perhaps the only representative. With Raimundo Amador it is possible to speak of a fusion. His combination of a background in Gypsy flamenco and improvisational styles–blues and jazz–has given him a sound and 'feeling' unique today in the world of flamenco.

FLAMENCO POP

The most widely known representative of flamenco pop is the band *Ketama*, made up of the Gypsy brothers Juan (b. 1965) and Antonio Carmona (El Camborio b. 1960), sons of Juan Habichuela,[206] and their cousin José Miguel Carmona (b. 1971), son of Pepe Habichuela. Ketama's success is founded on a catchy fusion of flamenco style guitar riffs and salsa rhythms. Each of these Gypsies is an excellent flamenco musician in their own right, with Antonio Carmona said to be the best percussionist on the cajón.[207] Ketama began their career signing on to the label Nuevos Medios which actually invented the term Jovenes Flamencos, hence initially Ketama were marketed as such.

La Barbería del Sur, another band made up of young Gypsies, represent a similar style. The guitarist Juan José Suárez 'Paquete' (b. 1966) alternates appearances with La Barbería with his role as accompanist to Enrique and Estrella Morente and Esperanza Fernández among others, showing himself to be an extraordinarily sensitive musician in this role. As he is the son of flamenco cantaor Ramón El Portugues (b. 1948) from whom Camarón took inspiration, his upbringing and musical background is rooted in flamenco, like the Carmonas of Ketama. El Negri (Enrique Heredia Carbonell b. 1972) also of La Barbería appears regularly in concert and on disc with Enrique Morente. Another popular Gypsy based band Navajita Plateá, formed by two Gypsies from Jerez have also established themselves as pop-flamencos. They participated on Moraíto Chico's 1999 CD *Morao Morao*. The essential ingredient for the success of these flamenco-pop bands, seems to be the Gypsy element which lends the productions an 'aire', a flavour that is shared by flamenco.

Others who fall under this umbrella are El Barrio (b. 1970) who started his career as a flamenco guitarist, something which heavily influences his singer-songwriter style, José El Frances, Manzanita and La Niña Pastori. José El Frances (born in France in 1971, hence his nickname José The Frenchman) sings a flamenco-pop style with a sweet delivery and flamenco ornaments. His ballads and suggestive stage manner made him an instant success with the Nuevos Medios label, but he does not sing in either flamenco compás nor with a flamenco emotional delivery. Accused of drug trafficking, his early success was cut short by a prison sentence as well as his own addiction. Time will tell whether he succeeds in shaking off this bad image and manages to join the mainstream once again. Manzanita (b. 1956 José Manuel Ortega Heredia) is a member of the Ortega clan which produced the legendary cantaor Manolo Caracol, among others, and he began his career as a sought after guitarist in the tablaos of Madrid. Abandoning a promising future as a guitarist, Manzanita produced a solo album which brought him fame. Recently he has combined his lyrical pop vocal style with Cuban *son*.

---

[205] 1908-1973 See Chapter 11, "Who Were the Famous Guitarists?"
[206] See Chapter 11, "Famous Guitarists".
[207] See Chapter 15, "The Fourth Element".

Manzanita appears in the final number on Carlos Saura's movie Flamenco, with Ketama singing the words of one of García Lorca's most famous poems: Verde Que Te Quiero Verde to a rumba rhythm. La Niña Pastori has a solid cantaora background but she works in an overtly commercial style of flamenco-light. In Spain diet foods with low sugar content or saccharine are generally called 'light', and when transferred to other things it means they are lacking in substance or seriousness. Niña Pastori sings predominantly *rumbas* and *tanguillos* and with a pop oriented production has become a top selling artist within Spain.

CHAPTER 14: WHY ARE PEOPLE SHOUTING AT THEM WHEN THEY SING?

No live performance of flamenco would be complete without the encouraging calls from audience and fellow performers. Without these, a Flamenco feels exposed, alone and unappreciated. Within Gypsy culture, to be alone, or to be outcast from the tribe or clan is the worst possible punishment, and in Spanish culture generally, and very much in Andalucia, being alone is seen as undesirable. Coming across a lone person perhaps reading a book, a typical Spanish question would be: "What are you doing here, all alone?" So these cries of encouragement may stem from this cultural outlook as much as from the basic desire to support someone in a stressful moment. Being on stage is a nerve wracking experience, to bare one's soul once up there is even more exposing, but it's precisely what is appreciated in flamenco. Fellow artists are aware of the performer's suffering and show their solidarity verbally.

Such shouts and murmurs are called *jaleos*[208] from the verb "jalear", to animate and encourage, which itself is a speciality within flamenco. But to call encouragement in the wrong place is scorned. So is hand clapping (*palmas*) in spontaneous accompaniment. Palmas is really an art in itself and has a context which the uninitiated 'outsider' can't appreciate. Audience participation doesn't have the same meaning in flamenco as in a pop or rock concert. Shouting appreciation from a crowd is normal throughout Spain–appreciation, and the opposite: insults. The Spaniard is not coy when it comes to expressing his or her approval or disapproval, in my experience the Spanish audience is one of the best: unlike audiences in most other countries where polite applause, deserved or not, is the norm, you can always tell whether a Spanish audience appreciates you or not.

Cries of *olé*–the quintessentially Spanish yell of encouragement and appreciation–accompany both flamenco and bullfighting. When the legendary bullfighter Curro Romero retired in 2001, his *mozo de espadas* (sword bearer) was asked, "Did you ever say anything to Curro as he went into the bullring, ever give him advice?" The *mozo* replied, "The only thing I ever said to Curro was *olé*." The word comes from the Arabic *wa-allah a*nd the English translation may be 'Good God!'

Other *jaleos* include: *Arsa!*   an untranslatable term peculiar to flamenco and sometimes used to encourage a donkey or horse to get going; *Eso es!* -'that's it!', *Asi se canta*- 'that's the way to sing!', *toma!* 'there you go!', and other more spontaneous shouts. Cries from the audience and fellow performers on stage are a vital part of flamenco. They show appreciation for a moment of emotional truth. *Agua!* (water) and *azúcar!* (sugar) are also common cries, perhaps relating to the Moorish culture in which both of these commodities are signs of wealth. In performances where more than two artists appear on stage, you'll often hear these cries to encourage the singer and guitarist, whether or not they're justified by the performance, to help create atmosphere and maybe make up for the coldness of the audience. Some of the most moving moments can be those of mutual appreciation between a *tocaor* and *cantaor* when a guitarist, deeply involved in his playing, is moved and inspired by the singer he is accompanying to murmur encouragement under his breath.

The living legend La Paquera de Jerez likes to establish communication with her audience. La Paquera is one of the most popular and venerated Flamencos and the audience at Madrid's 2000 Autumn Flamenco Festival were devoted to her, even before she began singing. Striding on stage in her characteristic gate, coming to the microphone as though it were an animal to be tamed, she asked in her booming voice: "Good Evening Madrid, how are we tonight?" To which an appreciative cabal in a seat behind me answered in an intimate voice: "We're in heaven."

---

[208]Jaleos is also a flamenco style, basically a rowdy bulerías, named after the popular term for a chaotic situation: 'un jaleo.'

CHAPTER 15: PATRIARCHS FOR A NEW MILLENNIUM

WHAT IS FLAMENCO NUEVO?

To judge from the variety of CDs stacked under the heading *Nuevo Flamenco* or *Flamenco Nuevo* in the stores, you'd think that all it takes to qualify is to add palmas and a flamenco guitar to the average Spanish pop band. A rumba, a tango and 'Bob's your uncle'. Certainly if they play in a flamenco compás then it will be flamenco. But as anyone who has witnessed good and bad flamenco will know, it takes more than simply a rhythmic cycle to make it so. Knowledge and experience of the traditions and styles adds an element which can't be faked. Basically, the performers themselves must be *flamencos* if it's to have that unique feeling.

Flamenco is the musical product of a fusion of cultures. It is one of the world's youngest art forms and is constantly evolving, developing fashions and experimenting with the unusual, some of which sticks-like the cajón, saxophone and flute-and some of which hasn't yet become widely accepted, like the cello, or Joaquin Cortes's skirt.[209] Only time and Flamencos themselves will reveal which experiments are adopted and eventually accepted as part of flamenco. There's nothing new with its flirtation with supposedly non-traditional instruments and styles. Already in the 1930s the famous guitarist Ramón Montoya was recording *soleares* accompanying the saxophone player Ricardo Vilches, who simply took the role of a cantaor, playing a single line vocal melody. Today, José Menese, who considers himself a purist and an orthodox cantaor, can often be seen singing to a cello accompaniment. It's a mistake to think of instruments such as the violin or piano as 'new' instruments in flamenco. During the era of the Cafés Cantantes, the dancers were accompanied not only by guitars, but also bandurrias and even violins. The piano has been common in Flamenco families and used as an accompanying instrument since the days of Opera Flamenca. The best known flamenco violinist Bernardo Parrilla, comes from a long line of Gypsy Flamencos[210], one of whom was a pianist. But the most exciting and recent evolution in flamenco has been in percussion with the addition and incorporation of percussive instruments such as the djembe and cajón.

One characteristic of Nuevo Flamenco is a sweetening of the vocalisations. The raw primitive cry is rare in the 'flamenco-light' songs which are included under this heading. A more accessible and amiable presentation, more commercial, is even adopted by cantaores *rancios*[211] such as José Mercé: *"Now I am making flamenco that is accessible. It must be universal, for everyone ... Now anyone who wants to can go to a flamenco concert and you don't need to know it or understand it. The beautiful part is that you feel it."*[212] Flamenco in this style has less force, less bone-marrow as a Spaniard would say and is reduced to the purely sensory aspect; i.e a catchy rhythm and melody.

FLAMENCO'S GENERATION X

Flamenco Nuevo is where flamenco catches up with the 21st century. Today's young performers, sometimes called Los Jovenes Flamencos, sometimes Los Nuevos Flamencos, are simply interpreting flamenco from the context of their experience. Flamenco's 'Generation X' grew up in an Andalucía freed from the social and psychological shackles of Franco's dictatorship, in towns and cities which quickly absorbed the trappings of foreign cultures far removed from flamenco. Sex & Drugs & Rock & Roll, Salsa, World and pop music

---

[209]This bailaor has a stage number where he appears dressed only in a bata de cola, a dress with a long train.
[210]Son of the guitarist Parrilla de Jerez, nephew of El Borrico.
[211]"Well-aged" or "mature," indicating a deep knowledge of flamenco's fundamentals.
[212]*Newsweek,* February 12, 2001.

were just some of the foreign elements which influenced them. Washing machines, refrigerators, TV, jet travel, and a lot of tourists eager to find the essence of Spain (which some believed must be in flamenco), surrounded them and these influences had to be incorporated into a way of life, a rhythm of living which was established in a previous century. How relevant could working in a mine be to an 18 year old Camarón singing *por tarantas*, hooked on heroin, driving from one recording studio to another? How meaningful could the traditional complaints of a starving Gypsy, forced to beg for crusts of bread, be to a Gypsy clan whose patriarch received a social security payment and who owned a night club on the edge of town? It wasn't that suddenly all marginalised families had a decent income and were able to wash their clothes in a washing machine rather than the river, or that all begging could cease (for many people it's still a regular source of income). But the changes which came so quickly after Franco's death in 1975 obviously had an effect on flamenco as an expression of identity.

The Flamenco generation of the 1960s started experimenting with all the outside influences they saw on TV and heard on the radio and on LPs. In the early 70s the rock group Smash upset flamencos and rock fans in equal measure by trying to invent an 'Andalucian Rock' using flamenco forms. Smash showed their contemporaries that Andalucia has its own style, closely identifiable with flamenco, and distinct from The Beatles influenced pop, or best-selling Spanish singer-songwriters like Joan Manuel Serrat. One of its founding members, Gualberto went on to accompany Agujetas, today considered one of the last guardians of *el cante puro*, using the sitar, the Indian instrument John Lennon is credited with introducing to a wider audience in the West.[213] This was just one of many attempts to 'reunite' el Cante Jondo with Indian music. Smash's efforts are sometimes cited as the beginning of the current era of flamenco-pop represented by such successful bands as Ketama and La Barbería del Sur. Both groups include Gypsies from flamenco dynasties in their line-up but neither group is flamenco.

Paco de Lucía is the Godfather of flamenco's Generation X. At a time when groups like the Rolling Stones and electric guitar wizards were the teenage Spaniard's heroes, Paco de Lucía's lightening fast *picado* matched the licks of any electric guitarist. His playing had the same driving force and hint of rebelliousness, and it fit in perfectly with the emerging local pop culture and experimentation, but in a language Andalusians could identify with.

He is responsible for the assimilation into flamenco of jazz chords, Brazilian harmonies and rhythms, the cajón, and the pre-chord *golpe* (percussive tap on the top of the guitar unique to flamenco), amongst other things. Because of him, the saxophone and flute, bass guitar and extensive percussion are all now expected elements in a modern flamenco concert. Other instruments such as the trumpet or cello have been introduced into flamenco because Paco opened up the field.

"When you ask Paco why he formed his sextet with those instrumentalists he'll answer that if Jorge Pardo had played the trumpet, for example, today everybody would be saying My God! The trumpet! What a flamenco instrument!"[214]

ICONS OF NUEVO FLAMENCO

The meeting between the young cantaor Camarón de La Isla, (1954-1992) and Paco in 1969 was a meeting of spirits. For most commentators on flamenco, this was the most important moment in the history of flamenco of the past quarter Century. The Gypsy cantaor from the Isle of Sanlúcar de Barrameda in the province of Cádiz, Andalucía, is the cantaor who has had the most impact on el cante in the recent history of

---

[213]see Chapter 13, "What is Flamenco Fusion?"
[214]Jorge Pardo, *Historia Guía del Nuevo Flamenco*, 1994.

flamenco. Paco and Camarón were *almas gemelas* (soul twins) who produced landmark recordings on which one can still hear the sparks fly. The cantaor, an amateur guitarist, fell in love with Paco's playing, and the guitarist, a frustrated cantaor, found his ideal in Camarón's style:

"Paco's father used to come often to Torres Bermejas[215]. One day, he brought his son with him. We understood each other quickly. He liked my stuff and I liked his. How was I not going to like it! He was a monster! During the time we worked together we understood one another by telepathy."[216]

As Paco reminisced:

" He always used to call me for each recording, although I couldn't always record with him. With me he felt safe, he knew I would bring out the best in him. I never let him get away with anything, and that gave him confidence. Sometimes I was a bit too demanding, but in the end he was grateful. I think I was the only person he paid attention to, like his big brother. We had a lot of respect for one another. He was such a genius of an artist... he could allow himself the luxury of doing whatever he pleased."[217]

Theirs was one of the most musically satisfying partnerships in the entire history of flamenco. During their collaboration which lasted on and off throughout Camarón's life, these two *monstruos* created an entirely new style of performance. A new *aire* crept into flamenco which has left an indelible mark on every cantaor and tocaor since. Camarón de La Isla did nothing to change the basic styles, but he revolutionised the delivery and the interpretation, connecting with a younger generation and opening the field of flamenco to bass guitars and drums. All Flamencos since Paco de Lucía and Camarón have aimed to follow in their footsteps, with the exception of those who made their careers outside Spain (Britain's Paco Peña or Juan Martín, or America's Juan Serrano for example, none of whom have successfully adopted the harmonies introduced by Paco de Lucía.)

Camarón de la Isla died at the age of 41 from lung cancer, but his well known addiction to heroin and other drugs led many people to attribute his death to the effects of these. He was also a heavy smoker. Paco Cepero, the Gypsy guitarist from Jerez who was Camarón's accompanist during the early stages of his career, recalls Camarón, then about 7 years old, approaching him in the Venta Vargas with a cigarette dangling from his lips. It's said he inhaled heroin rather than injecting, since he had a phobia of needles, which no doubt contributed to the development of his disease. His 'classic' Gypsy upbringing (no formal schooling, forced to work to survive at an early age) is the stuff of legend. As a child Camarón used to sing on the tramways of his home town, with his friend the cantaor Rancapino, for a few pesetas. Ramon de Algeciras, Paco de Lucía's brother (and, after his father, also his teacher) also accompanied him during 6-7 years. Camarón used to run off secretly to the famous Venta Vargas to hear his idol Caracol, who was:

"The only one who really touched me, he was one of those monsters you only get once in a while in history. Everything he sang sounded mature, but it touched you. I think that's the same gift I have. Caracol was one of those artists who rebelled against everything. He had his things, his peculiarities, but all the great cantaores have been strange. On top of this, he was the most generous, he was the only one who distributed money among the artists in the ventas."[218]

---

[215]The Madrid Tablao where Camarón worked in his early days.
[216]El Europeo N° 33 June 1991 "Camarón de La Isla: Duende" F. Rivas & José Candado
[217]El Mundo Magazine 1993 Interview by Ana Buenos
[218]El Europeo N° 33 June 1991

FLAMENCO ESSENCE

La Leyenda del Tiempo, the L. P. named after a poem by García Lorca which Camarón sings to a jaleos[219] rhythm, was the beginning of the Camarón legend. The album was produced in a similar style to that of a rock recording. Camarón is accompanied by bass guitar, drums and keyboard, while singing the verses of Lorca, Omar Khayam and non-traditional lyricists. It was the first time he had recorded without Paco de Lucía and it was the start of his partnership with Tomatito, a Gypsy guitarist from Almería who became his accompanist until the cantaor's death. Released in 1978, La Leyenda del Tiempo is still held as an example of inspiration, audacity and flamencura. It took many years before the diehards, clinging to their *Mairenismo*[220] and concept of flamenco purity, recognised that almost every Flamenco since Camarón has been influenced by this record and the ideas behind it. For many, it marks the beginning of Flamenco Nuevo, and introduced many aficionados, including me, to the poems of García Lorca. The track "Volando Voy", an infectious up-beat rumba by Kiko Veneno, who had stumbled across the world of flamenco via his partnership with the guitarist Raimundo Amador[221] became the hymn of that generation. Along with Paco de Lucía's spur of the moment rumba "Entre Dos Aguas", this recording remains the landmark in modern flamenco, the point from which all else departs.

Like flamenco legends before him, Camarón's vocal quirks and innovations have been incorporated into every cantaor's repertoire. He sang '*rin tin tin, a la bim bom bera*' in *Tangos Extremeños* he picked up from Ramón el Portugues and so everybody else began singing this chorus, along with his distinctive 'lailo lailo' vocalisations from a 1970s tangos. In 1977 he sang '*mira que mira mira*' in a chorus of voices which has now become standard in flamenco.

Camarón's voice is imbued with the essence of flamenco, that painful sound which comes not from poor intonation, but from something intangible and inexplicable which we can only label *flamencura* . Like his friend Enrique Morente, Camarón often sang long phrases, melismas which left you breathless from the tension he could build, and invariably drew *olés* and gasps of admiration from his audiences. Every palo he tackled became infused with his personal interpretation and style, which most aficionados and cabales described as adding majesty and distinction. Camarón knew instinctively how to build the tension and release of his bulerías, like a well trained composer–a quality he shared with Paco de Lucía, whose instinctive sense of musical structure (he has never studied formal composition) can be compared to any classical guitar composer's. Camarón's enigmatic personality, his Gypsy character and life style, combined with his flamenco instincts made him a natural object for idolatry. Even when he sang badly, which towards the end of his life was often, he was deemed to have given something worthwhile to the audience by his mere presence.

Memories such as this abound in the world of flamenco:

"If I remember rightly, it was in 1983. The now burnt-out Sports Palace of Madrid was the venue for its annual flamenco festival, and Camarón had closed the first half to great acclaim. The second half was just finishing when Angelita Vargas and el Biencasao brought out their little boy to dance por bulerías. This kid, about seven years old carried himself with natural grace. Suddenly a commotion among the audience alerted us to the timid presence of Camarón on stage. He'd come out, already in his street clothes, to sing to that little boy, to give him his blessing. Beside him, Tomatito watched, speechless. Then Camarón's voice broke with intensity and the boy transcended himself. Stamp stamp, he planted his feet. Madness broke out.

---

[219]An old style of flamenco dance, related to the soleá and the bulerías

[220]Named after Antonio Mairena's concept of Purity in flamenco

[221]See Chapter 13, "What is Flamenco Fusion?"

When all eyes turned to look for Camarón, the darkness of the stage curtain had swallowed him up. The sparkle remained, and then the amazement. The magic still hasn't worn off. It wasn't an apparition but a revelation. It makes me mad to think that not even a bit of a photo captured that, as far as I know, but me, I was there and I saw it, I swear to you I never felt the greatness of that Gypsy so close; pain and glory given up at the feet of a child."[222]

The mere fact that Camarón could fill such a huge venue shows how far flamenco had come. Instead of confined to the back rooms of restaurants and clubs, the new generation could draw crowds from outside the flamenco aficionado spectrum. In 1990 at the same venue, Camarón once again proved the strength and depth of his genius:

"With Camarón; the usual: the tumult, the yelling, the throwing yourself into the fiesta as though into an open tomb. He sits down, he 'tunes up' por alegrías and once again the clamour is released. His whole recital was like that, interrupted every so often by the public, who were already unconditional supporters. For an hour he sang enthusiastically but also with that incredible sagacity that makes him a figure apart in today's flamenco. Because, apart from the sociological phenomenon he generates in every appearance, the truth is that Camarón is a virtuoso of the best cante which he knows marvelously well and interprets with depth and intensity, and he communicates like no one else."[223]

For José Mercé, Camarón is responsible for bringing flamenco to a wider audience:

"When we were young, 30 years ago, we were treated like whores; we were the private singers to the 'señoritos', the play-boys, the marginalised. Since Mairena and Sordera, and above all Camarón, flamenco has gained a lot of dignity. Now everything is up to us; we finish a recital and can do whatever we feel like, we don't have to put up with anybody or look for earnings in the ventas. It's a different game. Now, we even get up at nine in the morning to go to the radio station and the multinationals promote us. Before, you'd make a record and nobody would notice."[224]

BEYOND FLAMENCO

At the time of Camarón's death, I was in Cordoba attending the guitar festival and chatting with the Brazilian classical guitar duo The Assad Brothers. Both of them knew of Camarón and lamented his death. He was a flamenco with international recognition. Camarón was admired by many artists from different disciplines outside flamenco, from Alfredo Kraus through Leonard Cohen and on to Mick Jagger and Bono of U2. For the French press Camarón was the 'Joe Cocker of San Fernando'. His last album was released posthumously, recorded while unknowingly in the final stages of his cancer. *Potro de Rabia y Miel*[225] was a labour of love for all concerned: *"He was very ill. It was very hard work. It seemed like José would break with each cry. We waited for hours and hours until he felt alright. But it turned out beautifully."*[226] With the tragically premature death of his *compadre* Camarón, Paco de Lucía was plunged into a deep depression which he finally purged himself of with his 1998 CD *Luzía* in which he pays moving tribute both to Camarón and his deceased mother, Luzía. The spectacle of Camarón's multitudinous funeral, with the equally legendary bullfighter Curro Romero and Paco de Lucía as pall bearers, and Gypsies ripping their shirts crying "please don't go", was moving testimony to the depth and strength of this humble cantaor's qualities.

---

[222]Antonio Valentín, *Alma Cien* magazine, N° 30, 2001.
[223]A.A. Caballero, *EL PAÍS,* May 4th, 1990.
[224]El País, April 26th, 2001.
[225]Philips 512408-2, 1992.
[226]Paco de Lucía.

Profoundly moved by Camarón's death, Enrique Morente said:

"There hasn't been a sound like his before nor now. Whatever he sang he turned to gold. His capacity to communicate was astounding. It was a new sound in el cante. He had a trademark which will remain for eternity, Camarón has influenced all of today's cantaores, even me possibly, somehow without me knowing. You always get something good from artists such as him, and although I've got my own personality, it's undeniable that José's cante moved me, it touched me. We were like brothers. When he came to Madrid he would spend a lot of time in my house. He was a charming person. We spent unforgettable times together. He'd hardly speak with people he didn't know well, but with those he was comfortable with he could be funny and say some hilarious things. He always turned up at my house with a smile on his face."[227]

Although it's easy to de-mystify or rationalise many popular cultural icons by blaming such social phenomena on the media, or 'mob-culture', or simply blaming the commercialisation of everything, sometimes these figures really do have qualities which justify their status. Camarón was one such figure. His sense of compás and his unique *quejío* gave the traditional forms a modern feel. His *tangos* and *bulerías* may be his greatest legacy, having become the equivalent in modern flamenco of a disco beat in 1970's pop. Today in Candelas, the bar in Madrid where members of Ketama used to meet with Camarón and Paco de Lucía (among others) for late night flamenco jam sessions, people crowd around the tiny bar, deafened by the music of Camarón de la Isla and Paco de Lucía blaring like rock music from the PA system. Sitting, standing, leaning around the bar, they lip-sync to the words of 'Como El Agua', bobbing their heads to the *tangos* beat. If ever one doubted that flamenco is the new Rock & Roll, here is the proof. The generation which grew up with "Entre Dos Aguas" in the closing stages of Franco's regime: classical composers, stage and film actors, all gather here in their element with Paco and Camarón as the sound track to their lives.

NEW THEMES FOR OLD TUNES

José Mercé, a Gypsy *cantaor* known for his orthodox style, sings: *"Alkaline batteries for my tired heart, alkaline batteries or I shall die desolate, alkaline batteries for the people I have lost, to give me a moment of happiness..."*[228] The words are by Vicente Amigo, the guitarist currently making the most impression on flamenco, and a perfect example of Flamenco Nuevo. *Caminos Reales del Cante*[229], Mercé's first CD, has one bulerías and a selection of 'jondo' styles such as the tarantos, soleá de Jerez, tientos and seguiriyas. His second CD 'Del Amanecer', produced by Vicente Amigo,[230] has three bulerías, one alegrías, a tango, and a flamenco-song based on the tanguillos rhythm, with a soleá and cartagenera thrown in as though as an afterthought. The faster, catchy rhythms of a *tanguillos* (a fast tango, not the same as the Argentinian tango) or a *bulerías* or *alegrías*, provide a groove, which doesn't demand any effort or emotional involvement from the listener. Many Latin American rhythms including Cuban son, salsa, rumba, colombiana, guajira, and milonga have been assimilated into flamenco and are considered more frivolous, less emotionally demanding to sing and easier for instrumentalists from other disciplines like jazz, rock, pop or classical to pick up.

The words evolve, just as life does. In the past, there were words sung about dying from gangrene or from typhus, and there were sometimes graphic descriptions of seeing a loved one carried off in the grave digger's cart, and asking the grave digger to cover her face.[231]

---

[227]www.flamenco.com
[228]*Del Amanecer* CD, Virgin 8468332
[229]Pasarela CDP1/571.
[230]Virgin 8468332.

El carro de los muertos	As the death cart
Pasó por aqui	Came by this way
Como llevaba la manita fuera	Her little hand was sticking out
Yo la conocí	And I recognized her

There were words about seeing a loved one thrown in the communal grave, and lamenting how soon the worms would be eating the mouth once kissed by a lover:

Diez años despues de muerto	Ten years after your death
y e gusano comió	And eaten by worms
letreros tendrán mis huesos	There will be signs on my bones
der tiempo que t'he querío	Of the years I have loved you

These are unlikely themes in 21st Century Spain.

Flamenco is restricting for those whose musicality goes beyond the confines of compás and the typical patterns of flamenco modes. Within flamenco there are plenty of cantaores and guitarists who feel the need to stretch their own boundaries, and because they are so fundamentally 'Flamenco'- everything they do has the distinct 'aire flamenca'- they stretch the boundaries of flamenco too. Others simply cross over into other areas, such as pop or Spanish ballad style, like Isabel Pantoja or Chiquetete. This makes it hard sometimes to distinguish between them and flamenco. Camarón explained: *"I've always tried to do new things, different, bring something of mine without losing the roots. Each new record of mine I hear the same thing over again, that it's not flamenco. I reply that everything I do is flamenco for the simple reason that I, by nature, above all, am flamenco and a Gypsy."*

In a 1993 interview[232] Paco de Lucia was asked whether flamenco was losing its origins *desmadrando*– becoming a mess, with all these innovations. He replied: *"Yes, but it doesn't matter, the waters always return to their level. Some wonderful adventures come from these crazy experiments. Flamenco will always be there, and absorb the positive things from every one of them. So long as out of every ten madnesses there's one good thing, that's all it takes. I think it's great that there are a bunch of lunatics out there!"*

The *cantaor* Enrique Morente (Granada,1942) is to this day perhaps the most adventurous 'New Flamenco'. He's orthodox in his study and knowledge (*afición*) of the *cante* but he's nevertheless the most *unorthodox* in his experimentation, singing the verse of Leonard Cohen, and turning Federico García Lorca into the most flamenco of poets. He has been called the 'Van Morrison del Albaicín'[233]. His regular accompanists are founder-members of the rock/pop group La Barbería del Sur, who all come from Gypsy flamenco dynasties themselves. Whether one considers Enrique Morente's version of Leonard Cohen's 'Priest'[234] as flamenco, when juxtaposed by Curro Malena's *livianas* on his CD *Carbon de Caña*[235] is a subjective choice. Both abide by the prescribed compás, and both cantaores have traditional flamenco voices, full of pain and resignation. And each remain fundamentally flamenco, since this is their grounding and experience, their way of being.

[231]A. Machado y Alvarez 'Demófilo': *Colección de Cantes Flamencos.*
[232]Magazine, *El Mundo.*
[233]The old Gypsy quarter and flamenco neighbourhood of Granada.
[234]*Omega* CD, El Europeo Musica 001.
[235]Ethnic B6793.

THE FOURTH ELEMENT

Percussion is big in Nuevo Flamenco. Since Paco de Lucía's percussionist Rubem Dantas and Ketama's Antonio Carmona started using the *cajón*, a percussive wooden box originally from Peru, it's become the most popular flamenco instrument after the guitar. Paco de Lucía's band discovered the cajón during a reception in Peru. Antonio Soler, the bailaor who was accompanying him on tour at the time recalls:

Rubem Dantas was playing the conga and I was playing the bonguito, and a group arrived playing the cajón, which was more dignified for flamenco. The first one to record it was Rubem, the next Ketama, Antoñito using Rubem's cajón too, and from there it started to appear on all the records and it started getting popular. You can't really credit me. Either way it was Rubem and Antonio Carmona– they know what they're playing with. From there on the cajón has really developed.[236]

The box of the cajón has a laminated side which rattles when it's struck. As Jorge Pardo explains:

"The problem with the drums in flamenco is that the skins have a vibrating note which muddles the precise rhythms in flamenco. And besides you have to hit them hard and they swallow up everything else. The cajón is easy, comfortable, it doesn't make a note, it's sort of between the palmas and the taconeo. It sounds like wood, like the golpes *on the guitar, it doesn't create too much harmony .... perfect."*[237]

The original Peruvian cajón is played in a different way. According to Pardo, Rubem Dantas created his own technique of playing the cajón. Now a flamenco cajón is considered a different instrument from the Peruvian original.

Percussive accompaniment to flamenco has developed beyond the traditional hand clapping (*palmas*) and finger snapping (*pitos*). *Palmas* is a unique accompaniment to flamenco styles using counter rhythms and polyrhythms, which the newcomer to flamenco sometimes find impenetrable. All *palmeros* -'hand-clappers'- use different tonalities by varying the area of the palm they strike according to the requirements of the style they're accompanying. The deeper, muffled sound of clapping both palms directly together is used in the slower, 'deeper' song styles, and usually only the singer will clap occasionally, as though to himself. It's a more subdued sound than the bright effect of fingers against the palm. Although the more exotic percussion instruments such as darbukas (also known as 'tabla') and the cajón have become the norm in flamenco recordings and recitals, it's still possible to find virtuosos in the traditional art of *palmas*, such as the Familia Montoya, or José Bandolero, Antonio Carbonell and Enrique Heredia 'Negri' who perform with Enrique Morente. In the Bienal de Flamenco de Sevilla, Manuel Soler teaches flamenco percussion. Many dance productions, such as those of Sara Baras and Joaquin Cortes, include a flamenco percussion solo. To the historical and traditional triumvirate of El Cante, El Baile and La Guitarra, a fourth element must be added; La Percusión.

EL NUEVO FLAMENCO PURO Opus 9?

We are often told by purists that true flamenco, the real cante jondo, el cante 'puro', consists of only three or four basic styles of cante. Purists by definition are traditionalists. Yet purity in an art form automatically means stagnation. In the words of Tom Waits: "All art must evolve. If it fails, then it wasn't worth it." Without an evolving interpretation, flamenco music would surely never have become as popular as it has in the past 50 years. But many flamencologists and aficionados lament the changes in modern flamenco. Again, there's nothing new in their fears and complaints since in 1881 Demófilo berated Silverio Franconetti for

---

[236]www.flamenco-world.com
[237]Historia-Guia de los Nuevo Flamencos

taking flamenco 'out of the caves' and into his café cantante. According to Demófilo this was the beginning of the end for cante jondo. Its primitive roots and the rawness of untrained voices was for him the only true representation of el cante gitano.

For about 50 years we've been asking the same questions of Flamencos and flamencologists: Is flamenco dead or dying? Will flamenco continue to exist if we write it down and teach it methodically? Purists always accuse innovators of endangering the essence of flamenco. They fear flamenco will be watered down and lose its fundamental power of expression, lose its identity because of the confusion with styles from outside traditional flamenco boundaries. The rapid growth in popularity of flamenco does indeed endanger the fundamental essence, as you can see from countless soul-less productions which seek to present flamenco as a mass market phenomena. But throughout its history flamenco has managed to present both the popular and the 'jondo' side by side. The new millennium is no different. If flamenco was originally a private art, expressing the 'pena' and hardships of a marginalised minority, this aspect of it has already been largely lost. Many of the traditional lyrics have no meaning for today's aficionados, and so flamenco is appreciated mainly for its sensory impact, the way the rhythms and singing style make you feel, not its social message. The universal qualities embodied in that sensory aspect still hold a fascination. The strength of emotion, the rhythmic and harmonic complexity still attract, making flamenco another globalised art form.

The addition of percussionists, saxophone, violin or flute players, bass guitar, cajón and backing vocals in a pop-chorus style, along with palmas and jaleos, make up many a Flamenco Nuevo production. The selection of cantes shows the modern direction flamenco has been taking for a generation: tangos/tanguillos, rumbas, alegrías and bulerías dominate. New mixtures of palos, tangos/bulerías and alegrías/rumba/tanguillos medleys with strong Latin American (particularly Cuban 'son') rhythmic slants are all the rage. The similarity with the era known as Opera Flamenca isn't hard to see.

Classical music (interpretations of the works of composers from the late 1800's) survives because of the variety of different interpretations of the scores. Beethoven's 9th will always sound like Beethoven's 9th, but classical music lovers-aficionados-can learn to distinguish between one interpretation and another, performed by different orchestras led by different conductors. Surely the version sanctioned by Beethoven would be the only 'pure' and authentic version? The persistent arguments about purity of form, must be self-defeating. In the words of Jorge Pardo, who describes flamenco as the product of a mixture of cultures:

There are flamenco melodies which are really Sefardic. They have Castillian rhythms, twists and turns and an Arabic vocal style, very Oriental, mixed with the unique Gypsy interpretation (...) And now they speak about 'flamenco puro'. Rubbish. It doesn't exist.[238]

But it's important to give early flamenco its proper context. Imagine the villages of Andalucía in the days of Silverio Franconetti (1823-1889). There was no TV, no radio, no telephones, no Walkmans nor CDs nor recorded sounds. It was impossible to imagine that one day a fast train would unite Madrid with Seville in just over two hours. There was no explosion of 'world culture' as we've experienced in the past 50 years. People didn't get to hear music from different countries as easily as today, and so whatever the inhabitants of those Andalucian villages sang, danced and played, was certainly pure and unique to that time. It surely was a simpler life, and the flamenco they sang and heard must have been more primitive than we can imagine, even with with the benefit of hindsight.

---

[238]*La Discoteca Ideal de Flamenco*, A.A. Caballero, Ed. Planeta 1995.

Flamencologists now in their 60s have had to accept Nuevo Flamenco and the addition of violins, flutes, and percussion to the flamenco stage despite their disapproval, since these elements have overwhelmingly been accepted by Flamencos and their public. A modern flamenco audience accepts dry ice and bulerías percussion solos as easily as aficionados of flamenco's 19th Century traditions accepted the exclusion of women at the ballot box.

In their day, the old masters such as Sabicas, Caracol, La Niña de Los Peines and Carmen Amaya were all considered revolutionary and 'new'. Therefore, in flamenco, if it's flamenco it can't be new, and if it's new, it can't be flamenco! The older generation laments that the roots are being lost, and that flamenco is no longer what it was. Well, neither is society, and flamenco merely reflects the changes experienced by those who are performing it. Perhaps reflecting their easier lives, today flamenco's express themselves with a *bulerías*, a *tango*, a *rumba*, or an *alegrías*, palos with catchy rhythms and an international appeal. El cante contains all of the fundamental human emotions and flamenco will survive because all of these feelings will be with us for as long as human beings are human beings. It's not necessary to understand the harmonic and modal secrets of each palo to feel moved by their emotional content. A scientific analyses of Paco's subtle rhythmic alterations to the basic patterns, or Camarón's spontaneous lengthening of the phrase, wouldn't change the fact that their musicality, although flamenco, crosses international, stylistic and cultural borders.

PLUS ÇA CHANGE....

The flamenco we see today in the festivals and shows promoted by record companies and artist's agents, is 'cleaned up', polished and presented according to the expectations of a respectable public. Because we are all so used to the sound of recorded perfection, we expect guitarists to have oceans of reverb and to play as fast and faultlessly as they do on their CDs. We expect singers to sit tidily on their chairs and sing in tune. We don't expect to see a drunken Gypsy throw up between his legs before spewing out a primordial, toneless stream of emotion, regardless of company. But this is really what flamenco comes from. El Pericón de Cádiz (1901-1980) recounted a time in the Seville fair when he and Manolo Caracol (1909-1973) got drunk together:

"One year, in the Feria de Sevilla I thought I'd go to Morillo's house on Barco street and when I got there I found Caracol's father, and after a bit his son arrived with some gentlemen who got stuck into the party. Later they called for Caracol to sing and a little bit after that, for me. I get there, I sit down, and there we were, singing until seven in the morning. Caracol, drunk, me, drunk, and as happens with wine, one of the gentleman who was nuts about Caracol, every time he sang would give him a couple of bills. So of course, since he didn't give me anything I said to him: 'Man! Let's see if there's anything for me!' And that offended him, we argued and he left the juerga so there we were just me and Caracol and a chap they called Lillo from Cádiz."

"At that hour, full of wine, it occurred to Caracol to go to his cousin's house, Rafael Ortega, and once we got there I remember he sent for Manolo de Huelva (guitarist). One bottle, another bottle, and after half an hour Manolo arrived, and he played and he played and we sang and we drank and after two hours like that, worn out, we went to the bar Postigo in the Alameda de Hércules and went into a room. Caracol asked for a bottle, and he's paying 'cause that's what he was like, when he had a couple of thousand pesetas in his pocket they were already spent. And me singing por alegrías with Manolo de Huelva accompanying me, singing and singing until once, Caracol was sitting with his head leaning on the table, throwing up everything he'd drunk. He raised his head and says to el Niño de Huelva: 'Manuel, play por seguiriyas.' And Manolo de Huelva plays por seguiriyas and Caracol comes up singing... May my children die, I swear I have never seen anything like

it! I was crying like a child, my hair standing on end listening to that man singing the way he sang that day after drinking I don't know how much wine and throwing up right there with his head between his legs..."[239]

You won't see that happening in a concert of Nuevo Flamenco, but you might see joints being rolled, and sometimes a gang fight between rival Gypsy groups. Violence and drugs accompany flamenco just as they do the rest of society. Since the margins of society produced what we're talking about, it's hardly surprising the bad elements of marginal groups still plague it.

During the VIII Festival Flamenco Caja de Madrid in 2000, I went to see Agujetas de Jerez sing for the first time. Agujetas is lauded as the purest representative of el cante jondo, the style Manuel de Falla and García Lorca (to name only the most famous supporters) believed to represent the purest state of grace of the Gypsy race. A state many feel an ordinary payo, non Gypsy, is incapable of attaining. This state, or characteristic ability of the race, seems to me to be a facility to let free rein of emotions and reactions spontaneously, without thinking how it might be received, nor what it means.[240]

Having been billed as the last to appear in an evening which began with Paco Cepero's solo flamenco guitar, followed by an interval, followed by José de La Tomasa, a more refined Gypsy cantaor from a legendary flamenco dynasty, Agujetas had plenty of time to work on the bottle of whiskey in his dressing room. And when he appeared, it showed. He walks in a gangly, loose limbed manner, the elderly Gypsy equivalent of a 'dude's swagger'. He gestured to his young guitarist proprietorially, ordering him to sit down and barely giving him time to adjust his tuning before launching into an opening 'temple'; testing his voice, warming up.

After each cante, he stood abruptly, often leaving the tercio half finished, and stepped adroitly away from his chair and microphone with something like a drunkard's agility, never once knocking over his little plastic cup of whiskey which he had brought on stage with him. During his cante, he would gesture to the guitarist in a way which made me feel he had no understanding of the guitarist's role with him. He made little movements of his hand, as though he were in control of what the guitarist was doing, ignoring the fact that the guitarist was following the accepted design of each form. He would nod as though to say, "Okay, you go ahead and do that, but slow down here and play quieter".

His first seguiriyas came to an abrupt end when he got tired of it, obviously losing inspiration in the way that only a Gypsy could get away with. He simply stood up and flapped his arms about in acknowledgment of the applause, sitting himself back down and shouting uneccessarily into the microphone by way of excuse, that he's old, after all. Having finished off his whiskey, he yelled unceremoniously back stage to get someone to bring him some more. In his thick Andaluz accent he cried out, saying he would even drink water, what the hell. What other kind of artist could get away with interrupting his own song for a sip of his drink, forcing the guitarist to repeat a phrase so the whole thing didn't fall apart? What other artist could do this in the middle of a blood curdling vocalisation, a lament on the death of his mother?

In his cante that night he did not reach any particular depth of emotion nor inspired embellishment. No more than countless other Gypsies I have seen. Despite his new found fame as the maximum exponent, as the last true guardian of the real cante puro, there was very little that night to warrant such fame. In hundreds of villages dotted around Andalucia and Extremadura there are countless, nameless, toothless old Gypsies and peasants, their faces scarred by knife fights, who can reach the same level of artless expressivity. It was not a good night for Agujetas. After all the hyperbole it appeared that when it comes down to it, all this maximum

[239]J.L Ortiz Nuevo; *Las Mil y Un Historias de Pericón de Cádiz.* Ediciones Demófilo, Madrid 1975
[240]See Chapter 12, "What Is Duende?"

exponent of the song in its purest form, is a drunken peasant with no social graces.

In Dominique Abel's 1998 film on Agujetas[241] one sees him in a more sober state, singing in a small charmless cafe room surrounded by men and women. The expression on the listener's faces reveals everything. It gives us the answer to the question: "What's the big deal?" Without exception, the sound of Agujetas' voice penetrates each listener and turns their consciousness inwards to follow it. Their faces are concentrated, an inward look in their eyes, an almost pained, sad expression. Some look as though they have glimpsed the very abyss with a resigned acceptance, each one seems to be acknowledging with an impotent "I know". The film captures something of Agujetas' famed ability to touch his listeners and express what we recognise to be our own emotions. In the words of Moraito, the Gypsy guitarist who accompanies him on film Manuel Agujetas' cante is: "something wild, in a state of purity. His cante sounds of the smithy, it smells of the smithy." Agujetas' cante is not practised in the classical sense, his is the spontaneous delivery of one whose art is not dressed up with refined mannerisms, not polished to a level of virtuosic perfection. In this kind of 'cante puro' the sense of recognition one finds is one of relief, and even release. We too, feel sad, melancholy, hatred, jealousy. We too, deep down, recognise that we're all 'in it up to here' despite our clean clothes. We're all 'in it up to here' emotionally. It is art in the sense that it shows us who we are, and anything which does that, is to be treasured.

---

[241]*Agujetas Cantaor,* Ideale Audience, 1998.

FLAMENCO GLOSSARY

A

* Aficionado/a   Someone who enjoys and studies flamenco in any sense, either as a participant or spectator. A good cantaor will also be said to be a buen aficionado, since he will also have studied the past masters and forms.

*afillá   A type of hoarse, earthy flamenco voice, coined to describe the quality of voice of El Fillo, a Gypsy cantaor from the late 1800's. A voice like El Fillo is una voz afillá. This term is sometimes confused with afilá which is the Andaluz pronunciation of afilada meaning cutting or sharp.

*Aflamencado/a   Describes a style of song which although not necessarily based on a flamenco compás, uses some musical elements or characteristics of flamenco. Generally it's used as a derogatory description of a song sung in pseudo-flamenco style.

*'alante   Andalucian pronunciation of *Por delante* "in front", also *P'alante* used to describe a cantaor whose singing is good enough to be center stage.

*'atrás   From por atras - behind. The Andaluz pronunciation is *p'atras*. Refers to singers who stand at the back of the stage, behind the dancer; *Un cantaor de atrás.*

*Andalucía   The largest region of Spain in the South comprising eight provinces; Huelva, Sevilla, Cádiz, Jaén, Málaga, Almería, Granada and Córdoba. The cities of Cádiz, Sevilla, Jerez and Huelva lay claim to the distinction as the birthplace of flamenco.

* Ay   Typical Spanish term which can be used in pain and happiness, in flamenco the Ayeo- literally the *Ays* - is when a singer sings using this one word, usually at the opening of his cante.

B

*baile   Flamenco dance

*bailaor   Male Flamenco dancer

*bailaora   Female flamenco dancer

*braceo   Graceful movement of the arms during the dance

C

*cabales   More than just an 'aficionado', a cabal is an expert on flamenco who can distinguish the many variations within the styles. The term is used generally in Andalucía to indicate someone or something which is honourable and just. It was also used to indicate when something was finished off, completed. In flamenco forms the cabal is a change from minor to major mode, characteristic of the Seguiriyas a cabal, for example.

*cajón	Percussive wooden box, originally from Peru.
*Caló	The original language of Spanish Gypsies, no longer spoken fluently. It is related to Hindi and Punjabi as spoken in the territories from which the Gypsies originated. Caló is not the same as the Rom language still spoken by the Central European Gypsies.
*cantaor	Male flamenco singer
*cantaora	Female flamenco singer
*cante	Refers exclusively to flamenco song. Canto is any other style of song
*cante chico /cante grande.	Literally 'little song' and 'great song'. These terms were coined in 1958 by the writer Juan Carlos de Luna who considered some flamenco forms to be less demanding than others. He was the first to make the distinction between *cante grande* and *cante chico*- "great song" and "small song"- a differentiation few flamencos support today.
*cante jondo	'Deep song' from the Spanish *hondo* meaning "deep", which in Andalucian dialect is pronounced *jondo*.
*cejilla	The capo fixed over the strings on the fingerboard by a guitarist to raise the tone of the instrument and adjust to the tessiture of the singer being accompanied.
*compás	Refers to the cyclic rhythm of many flamenco forms. The term is also used in music generally to denote a measure and these two different uses can cause confusion. The flamenco compás is the cycle of beats maintained throughout a given *palo*. To have *buen compás* is to have a good sense of flamenco.
*copla	A verse of flamenco song
*cuadro	Traditional name for the group of flamenco performers comprising guitarists dancers, singers and others.

D

*desplante	A section of a dance performed after the llamada. As in *desplante por bulerias*.
*duende	The Spanish term for 'ghost', it was first applied to flamenco by the poet Federico García Lorca to describe the trance-like inspired state of a performer.

E

*escobilla	Moment in el baile when the attention is focused on the feet, prior to a zapateado

F

*falseta   A melody played by the guitarist between verses of the song. Guitarists may base entire compositions on series of falsetas, and aficionados learn the falsetas of past and present masters to add to their repertoire.

G

*gachó   Non-Gypsy

*gitano   Spanish Gypsy originating in the Punjab area of Northern India and Pakistan

*golpe   A tap on the guitar's soundboard

J

*jaleo   From the verb 'jalear' which means to encourage. It's also used generally to refer to a complete mess: Que jaleo!

*jondo   Andalucian pronunciation of *hondo*-deep-used exclusively in relation to flamenco.

*juerga   A flamenco party. The Real Academia de La Lengua Española has determined the ety mology of this word to be from *huelga*-"to strike", as in stop work. It's interesting, however, to note that *jerga* in the Pushtu language (spoken in the territories between Afghanistan and India where Spanish Gypsies originated) means "a village gathering of elders to discuss and plan community matters." It's easy to imagine such meetings as rowdy and argumentative and even followed by a concluding song and dance–hence juerga ...?

L

*letra   The words to a song–lyrics.

*llamada   A moment in el baile signaling the start of the desplante. In the guitar, it is usually played as a chord change on the third beat of the compás.

M

*mantón (de Manila) Embroidered silk shawl with long fringes originating in Manila, the Philippines, which was first captured by the Spanish in 1571.

P

*palillos   'Little sticks;' the Andaluz diminuitive of *palos*- the primitive precursos to the castanets. It's possible the flamenco term palos stems from the sticks originally used to keep the rhythm.

*palmas   Palms of the hand- literally means "clapping"

*palmeros   Those who accompany flamenco with palmas.

*payo   cf. gachó: Another term for non-Gypsies, possibly from paysano - countryman or peasant.

*pitos   Snapping fingers

Q

*quejío   "Complaint" or "lament"- from *quejarse*- "to complain"

R

*rasgueado From *rasgar*–"to scratch," a guitar strumming technique

S

*sonanta   Refers to Flamenco song and music, most often to the guitar

*soniquete A Flamenco feeling and sound

T

*tablao   Andaluz pronunciation of *tablado*–a stage. Today it is exclusively a restaurant/bar where flamenco shows are staged.

*tocaor   The flamenco term for a guitarist

*tacon   Shoe heel

*taconeo   Foot tapping in flamenco baile involving mainly the heel

*toque   Guitar playing

Z

*zapateado Fast heel-toe alternation in the baile. Usually thought to derive from the word zapato meaning shoe. However, in Morroco and other Arab speaking countries the word 'zapa' is used to frighten away cats, in Spain to *zapear* means to frighten away cats. Such a fierce dance would do it!

RECOMMENDED LISTENING

This is by no means an exhaustive list of flamenco recordings but would make a good start for a collection. No flamenco collection can do without something by Paco de Lucía and Camarón de La Isla, and if you're interested in the developments these two latter day masters have initiated, some older recordings will fill in the gaps and illuminate the path they have followed. As Paco de Lucía is widely considered the all time greatest flamenco in history, a complete collection of his works is recommended. Most of it has been reissued in boxed collections of three volumes each by Mercury.

PACO DE LUCIA:

-Concierto de Aranjuez de J. Rodrigo
Philips/Polygram Iberica 510 301-2
© 1991

- Interpreta a Manuel de Falla
Philips/Polygram Iberica 836 032-2
© 1978

-La Fabulosa Guitarra de Paco de Lucía
Philips/Polygram 842 954-2
©1967

-Fantasía Flamenca
Philips/Polygram Iberica
© 1969

-Fuente Y Caudal
Philips/Polygram 832340-2
© 1973

-Paco de Lucía en Vivo desde El Teatro Real
Philips/Polygram Iberica 838 381-2
© 1975

-Almoraima
Philips/Polygram Iberica 832022-2
© 1976

-Solo Quiero Caminar
Philips/Phonogram 810 009-2
© 1981

-Passion Grace & Fire
With John McLaughlin and Al Di Meola
Philips/Phonogram
© 1983

-Siroco
Mercury/Phonogram 830913-2
© 1987

-**Zyriab**

Philips/Polygram Iberica 846707-2

© 1990

-**Live in America** Excellent sample of the septet which includes Jorge Pardo and Carles Benavent mixing straightforward flamenco with jazz-flamenco

©1993

-**Luzia**

Mercury/ Polygram Iberica 558 165-2

© 1998

CAMARÓN DE LA ISLA: As with Paco de Lucía, most of Camarón's recordings have been reissued in boxed sets which should be in any flamenco collection.

All Polygram/Philips

-**Castillo de Arena**

© 1977

La Leyenda del Tiempo

© 1979

-**Como El Agua**

©1997

-**Antología 3CD set**

Mercury © 1996

CANTAORES:

MANUEL TORRE Legendary Gypsy cantaor who seems to have embodied all that is Flamenco
-La Leyenda del Cante
©Sonifolk 20146

LA NIÑA DE LOS PEINES No flamenco collection should be without an example of Pastora Pavón, for many the best cantaora of all time
-Voz de Estaño Fundido
Sonifolk ©1997

CARACOL
-Grands Cantaores du Flamenco Vol 7
©Le Chant du Monde Harmonia Mundi

TERREMOTO DE JEREZ
-Grands Cantaores du Flamenco Vol 4
©Le Chant du Monde

ENRIQUE MORENTE His roots are in the orthodox cantes of his forefathers, yet he is the most experimental and innovative of all present day cantaores, arousing strong criticism and fervent devotion in equal measure among aficionados.
-Cantes Antiguos del Flamenco
Hispavox 724383765522
©1969-1996
-Homenaje Flamenco A Miguel Hernández
Hispavox 7243 83765621
© 1971-1996
-Esencias Flamencas
Ethnic/Auvidis B 6151
© 1988
-Lorca
Virgin Chewaka 847030 2
© 1998
-Negra, Si Tu Supieras
Nuevos Medios 15602
© 1992
-Omega
El Europeo Música 001
© 1996

EL LEBRIJANO A highly influential cantaor whose career has passed through contrasting periods, from his beginnings as a main attraction in festivals through theatrical and operistic productions relating to the history of Spain's Gypsies, collaborations with North African musicians and ultimately 'fusions' with different musicians such as Bulgarian women's choir. Profoundly flamenco voice, if you can find some early recordings he has invariably been accompanied by top guitarists including El Niño Ricardo, Paco de Lucía, and Juan Habichuela

-Casablanca
EMI Hemisphere 7243 4 93342 29
© 1998
-Lagrimas de Cera
EMI 7243 5 2008322
© 1999
-Sueños En El Aire
Senador CD 02803
© 2001

CARMEN LINARES Simply the finest cantaora active today with profound flamencura, outstanding musicality and excellent knowledge of the forms. Everything she does is outstanding.
-La Luna en el Río
Ethnic/Auvidis © 1991
-Canciones Populares Antiguas
Auvidis ©1994
-Antología La Mujer en el Cante 2CDs One of the finest flamenco recordings of the past 50 years featuring accompaniment of some of flamenco's finest guitarists
Mercury/Polygram ©1996
-Un Ramito de Locura
©Mercury/Universalmusic 2001

RANCAPINO Childhood friend of Camarón de La Isla, excellent rajo voice and flamencura in an orthodox style which is hard to find in modern day recordings
BMG ©1996
Rancapino
Turner ©1995

LOLE Y MANUEL
-Una Voz Y Una Guitarra 2CDs live album which captures some of the old charm which brought this couple to fame in the 70s, and a good example of the Familia Montoya's prowess in Gypsy jaleos.
Virgin ©1995

JOSÉ MERCÉ Although he comes from an orthodox Jerez Gypsy dynasty of cantaores, Mercé is now one of the foremost representatives of Nuevo Flamenco thanks to his recorded collaborations with Vicente Amigo who shows a knack for producing commercially successful flamenco.

-Caminos Reales del Cante

©Pasarela 1987 Produced before his adoption by the Nuevo Flamenco 'movement' this recording shows Mercé's roots and orthodoxy which are more usual in his live appearances

-Del Amanecer

©Virgin 1998

-Aire

©Virgin 2000

PEPE DE LUCÍA Paco's brother, with whom he began his career as a child, an example of which can be found on *El Orgullo de Mi Padre*. Pepe de Lucía is one of the unsung great cantaores of his generation, perhaps because he has slipped into the role of producer of commercial-style flamenco for many younger cantaores. Some of his more orthodox style can be found in Hispavox's *Magna Antología*

-Magna Antología

-El Orgullo de Mi Padre

©Nuevos Medios 1996

DUQUENDE First solo album of this young Gypsy from Barcelona who toured with Paco de Lucía, representative of the Camaronero school of Nuevo Flamenco

-y La guitarra de Tomatito

Nuevos Medios ©1993

MIGUEL POVEDA

-Zaguán

© 2001 Harmonia Mundi

Third solo CD from this Barcelona cantaor shows the maturity and flamencura gained since winning the 33rd Lámpara Minera contest and all speciality prizes in 1993

ESTRELLA MORENTE- Enrique Morente's daughter, with whom she shares a profound flamencura and afición. Add to this her Gypsy heritage (her mother is Gypsy, Enrique Morente is not) which gives a certain edge, captured in her first solo CD which judiciously combines the traditional with the modern and superb accompaniment. Already considered an outstanding artist.

-Mi Cante y Un Poema

©Virgin 2000

-Calle del Aire

©Virgin 2001

COMPILATIONS AND ANTHOLOGIES

ANTOLOGIA DEL CANTE FLAMENCO 2CDs

Originally produced in France in 1954 under the directorship of guitarist Perico el del Lunar, this was the first collection of its kind and remains a landmark in the history of flamenco for its representation of old cantes which few modern day cantaores can sing. Reissued on CD minus the informative sleeve notes of the original -Hispavox ©1960/ 1988

MAGNA ANTOLOGÍA DEL CANTE FLAMENCO Box set of 10 CDs

The most complete selection of cantes from a wide range of artists, with informative sleeve notes from the leading Spanish flamencologist José Blas Vega; In Spanish only.
Hispavox © 1982

THE STORY OF FLAMENCO
EMI Hemisphere © 1997

Good, medium-priced compilation CD for exposure to some of the old masters.

GRANDES CANTAORES DEL FLAMENCO This set of compilation CDs from Philips are all worthwhile
-**Antonio Mairena**
-**Chato de La Isla**
-**La Paquera de Jerez**
-**Porrinas de Badajoz**
-**Juan Peña El Lebrijano**
-**Terremoto de Jerez**

FLAMENCO VIVO ETHNIC AUVIDIS Series of CDs produced under the direction of Frédèric Duval in

France, every recording in this series is worthy of attention. Focusing mainly on artists from Jerez, often representing the only recordings of cantaores who don't reach the mass media. The sleeve notes are authoritative funds of information in English and French on flamenco generally and the artists themselves.

-Curro Malena	"Carbon de Caña"	©1994
-Fernando de la Morena	"De Santiago a Triana"	©1994
-Tomasa La Macanita	"Con el Alma"	©1995
-Chano Lobato	"La Nuez Moscá"	©1996
-Ines Bacán	"Soledad Sonora"	©1998
-El Barrullo	"Plazuela"	©1995
-El Torta	"Colores Morenos"	©1994
-Rubichi	"Luna de Calobozo"	©1996
-Moraito	"Morao y Oro"	©1992

GUITARISTS

RAMÓN MONTOYA
-El Genio de la Guitarra Flamenca 2 CDS
Grabaciónes Historicas 1923-1936
©1999 Sonifolk

MANOLO SANLÚCAR
-Tauromágia
© 1998
-Locura de Brisas Y Trino
With Carmen Linares
© 2000 Mercury

PEPE HABICHUELA
-A Mandeli
© Nuevos Medios 1983/94
-Habichuela en Rama
© Nuevos Medios 1997
-& The Bollywood Strings
© Nuevos Medios 2001

VICENTE AMIGO
-De Mi Corazon al Aire
© CBS/Sony 1991
-Poeta
© CBS/Sony 1997

RAFAEL RIQUENI One of the most creative post-Paco de Lucía soloists his influence has been far reaching, despite frequent withdrawal from the flamenco scene. Can be heard accompanying Carmen Linares on Carlos Saura's Flamenco and her anthology of Mujeres en el Cante
-Juego de Niños
© Nuevos Medios (1986) 2000
-Mi Tiempo
© Nuevos Medios 1990

GERARDO NUÑEZ This guitarist made such a huge impact with his debut album *El Gallo Azul* in 1988 that his position at the forefront of the next flamenco guitar generation was assured. Despite somewhat limited compositional ideas (most of the falsetas and chords from *El Gallo Azul* return in subsequent recordings) Nuñez's strong musical personality, a flamencura strongly reminiscent of Paco de Lucía (with a kind of *rabia*-"anger" in his playing) and his technique are captivating. He is one of the finest representatives of flamenco-jazz while also being at home among the ranks of post Paco de Lucía flamenco guitarists.

-Flamencos En Nueva York

©1993

-Calima

©El Gallo Azul 1999

FLAMENCO-JAZZ

JORGE PARDO Of the musicians who came to flamenco from a jazz background, the flute and sax player Jorge Pardo, and the bass and mandola player Carles Benavent are the most influential. Both individually and as members of Paco de Lucía's sextet/septet they have developed a unique language of jazz-flamenco. Possibly the first real musical fusion since flamenco itself.

-Las Cigarras son Quizás Sordas

©Nuevos Medios 1991

-Velóz Hacía su sino

©Nuevos Medios 1993

CARLOS BENAVENT Often spelled "Carles", since he hails from Catalunya, this bass player has adapted flamenco techniques such as alzapúa to the fretless bass which all other players now emulate.

-Agüita que Corre

© Nuevos Medios 1991

WHY AREN'T THE GYPSY KINGS IN THIS LIST?

This group of French Gypsies (related to Manitas de Plata) comes from the South of France where flamenco is extremely popular, however they don't play flamenco. It is not simply because the Gypsy Kings are French that they are not invited to perform at any Spanish flamenco festivals, or classified as "flamenco" in specialist stores, but purely because they are NOT flamencos. Essentially, their style is limited to the rumba. Vocally and linguistically they are unique since they sing in a language which is neither French nor Spanish, and certainly not a flamenco dialect. Their success is due mainly to good marketing and catchy rhythms, and an exploitation of their Gypsy heritage. The adoption of themes such as *Bamboleo* by Spanish crooner super star Julio Iglesias helped their international image and sales.

VIDEOS

Some of these films are now available on DVD

-RITO Y GEOGRAFÍA DEL TOQUE

This series is compiled from the more extensive *Rito y Geografía del Flamenco* collection which is in Spanish with no subtitles. Contains interviews and voice over in Spanish with no subtitles, but the guitar playing needs no translations. Some historic footage of legendary players such as Diego del Gastor on video N° 5 make the whole collection worthwhile.

©ALGA Editores S.L

-AGUJETAS CANTAOR

Film by Dominique Abel, in Spanish with no subtitles filmed entirely in black and white until the closing image, beautifully captures this legend of el cante puro.

©1999 Ideale Audience

-SEVILLANAS by Carlos Saura. Although the Sevillanas is the folkloric song and dance from the province of Seville, it has long been established as a flamenco form. This beautiful movie depicts the folkloric as well as the flamenco Sevillanas including a must-see performance by Camarón singing to 'La Diosa' Manuela Carrasco and a duet by Paco de Lucía and Manolo Sanlúcar.

©1992 Juan Lebron Productions

-FLAMENCO by Carlos Saura. Simply the best movie ever made on the subject. Includes a selection of styles and artists representing most aspects of flamenco

©1995 Juan Lebron Productions

-LIGHT AND SHADE Documentary by Michael Meert on Paco de Lucía including his personal reminiscences and philosophy and some historic footage. A must have for all guitar fans. English voice over

©1995 MMG Video

BIBLIOGRAPHY

SPANISH:

ALMERÍA POR TARANTAS
        -Antonio Sevillano Miralles
Instituto de Estudios Almerienses de la Diputación Provincial de Almería 1996

ANTONIO MAIRENA SU OBRA, SU SIGNIFICADO
        -Fernando Quiñones
Editorial Cinterco 1989

CAMARÓN DE LA ISLA- EL DOLOR DE UN PRINCIPE
        -Francisco Peregil
El País Aguilar 1993

EL CANTE FLAMENCO
        -A.A. Caballero
Alianza Editorial 1994

COLECCIÓN DE CANTES FLAMENCOS RECOGIDOS Y ANOTADOS POR ANTONIO MACHADO Y ALVAREZ 'DEMÓFILO'
Portada Editorial Biblioteca Flamenca Nº1

ENRIQUE MORENTE LA VOZ LIBRE
        -Balbino Gutiérrez
SGAE 1996

ESCENAS ANDALUZAS 1847
        -Serafín Estébanez Calderón "El Solitario"
Navidad 1995

LA DISCOTECA IDEAL DE FLAMENCO
        -A.A.Caballero
Planeta 1995

GITANOS DE LA BÉTICA
        -José Carlos de Luna
Universidad de Cádiz 1951

GUÍA LIBRE DEL FLAMENCO
        -José Manuel Gamboa con la colaboración de Pedro Calvo
SGAE 2001

HISTORIA DEL FLAMENCO
Ediciones Tartessos 1995

HISTORIA GUIA DEL NUEVO FLAMENCO- El Duende De Ahorra-
        -Pedro Calvo
        -José Manuel Gamboa
Ediciones Guía de Música (Colcción La Encrucijada) 1994

LUÍS MARAVILLA "POR DERECHO"
    -Miguel Espín
    -José Manuel Gamboa
Fundación Machado/ Area de Cultura del Ayuntamiento de Sevilla 1990

MANUEL DE FALLA Y EL "CANTE JONDO"
    -Eduardo Molina Fajardo
Universidad de Granada 1998

MEMORIA DEL FLAMENCO I- II
    -Félix Grande
Espasa Calpe, S.A 1987

MUNDO Y FORMAS DEL CANTE FLAMENCO
    -Ricardo Molina
    -Antonio Mairena
Libreria Al-Andalus 1979

LA MÚSICA ARÁBIGO-ANDALUZA
    -Christian Poché
Ediciones Akal, S.A 1997

LOS NOMBRES ARTISTICOS EN EL MUNDO FLAMENCO-EL PORQUÉ DEL APODO Y DE LOS CAMBIOS DE NOMBRE-
    -Manuel López Rodríguez
Ediciones Giralda 1997

PACO DE LUCÍA CAMARÓN DE LA ISLA
    -Félix Grande
    -David González, *Zaafra*
Caja Madrid Lunwerg Editores 1998

PERICO EL DEL LUNAR- Un Flamenco de Antología
    -José Manuel Gamboa
Ediciones La Posada 2001

LA PRISIÓN GENERAL DE LOS GITANOS Y LOS ORÍGENES DE LO FLAMENCO
    -Antonio Zoido Naranjo
Portada Editorial Biblioteca Flamenca Nº6 1999

SEMILLAS DE ÉBANO EL ELEMENTO NEGRO Y AFROAMERICANO EN EL BAILE FLAMENCO
    -José Luis Navarro García
Portada Editorial Biblioteca Flamenca Nº 4 1998

SILVERIO REY DE LOS CANTAORES
    -José Blas Vega
La Posada 1995

TEORÍA DEL CANTE JONDO
    -Hipólito Rossy
CREDSA S.A 1966/1998

ENGLISH:

ANTONIO DE TORRES GUITAR MAKER- HIS LIFE & WORK
-José L. Romanillos
Element Books Ltd. 1987

GYPSIES AND FLAMENCO- THE EMERGENCE OF THE ART OF FLAMENCO IN ANDALUSIA
-Bernard Leblon
University of Hertfordshire Press 1995

GYPSIES- AN ILLUSTRATED HISTORY
-J.P Liégeois
Al-Saqi Books 1986

THE LEGACY OF MUSLIM SPAIN
-Salma Khadra Jayyusi. Ed.
Brill's Scholars' List

LIVES AND LEGENDS OF FLAMENCO
-Don Pohren
Society of Spanish Studies 1988

QUEEN OF THE GYPSIES- THE LIFE AND LEGEND OF CARMEN AMAYA
-Paco Sevilla
Sevilla Press 1999

SEGOVIA AN AUTOBIOGRAPHY OF THE YEARS 1893-1920
Macmillan Publishing Co., Inc 1976

SOUTH FROM GRANADA
-Gerald Brenan
Hamish Hamilton, London 1957